Home Offic

CW00957072

POLICE DOGS

Training and Care

London: Her Majesty's Stationery Office

© *Crown Copyright 1983*
First published 1963
Second edition 1973
Third edition 1983

ISBN 0 11 340781 5

Front Cover

Constable Ivor Morgan of the Surrey
Constabulary with his dog,
Mountbrowne Kestrel.

Kestrel, now aged 7, was bred for
police work by the Surrey
Constabulary in 1975. P.C. Morgan,
who has been a dog handler for 8
years, and Kestrel have been a very
successful operational team, both in
general police dog work and in the
specialist field of drugs detection.

Preface to third edition

When in 1963 the first edition of the Dog Training and Care Manual was published, the members of the Home Office Standing Advisory Committee on Police Dogs were only too conscious that experience would make it necessary for revised versions to be published from time to time to keep abreast of changing needs and current thinking.

The Committee in 1969 published a Review of Police Dog Training (PDC 101) which was a survey of all police dog training in England, Scotland and Wales, with recommendations for guidance for the future.

The Committee has been helped considerably by the advice and experience of the members of its Training Sub-Committee who regularly meet to discuss all aspects of police dog training. I should like to place on record our appreciation of the very real contribution towards the revision of the Manual made by these members who are all real enthusiasts and very knowledgeable about police dog work. We remain indebted to Mr R S T Boden MRCVS for his contribution to Chapter 16 'Health of Dogs'.

This Manual sets out the principles which govern the use of dogs in the police service. We have gone a long way since the early pioneering days. However, the basic objects for their use remain the same:

a Preventative and operational patrols
b Tracking
c Searching
d Recovery of articles at scenes of crime
e Locating children and missing persons
f Rowdyism.

There are other aspects of scent discrimination, outside the scope of this book for which dogs can be used. One of the most important of these is their developing use for seeking and recovery of drugs.

Police dogs are very much an integral part of the police service and to maintain our high reputation in the international police dog world, it is imperative that handlers and instructors continue to follow the principles laid down in the Training Manual.

With the sophisticated developments in training there is no doubt the book will have to be revised periodically. It is hoped that suggestions for additions and revisions will be sent to the Secretary, Home Office Standing Advisory Committee on Police Dogs, 50 Queen Anne's Gate, London SW1H 9AT.

SIR JAMES CRANE CBE
Chairman,
Home Office Standing Advisory Committee on Police Dogs

December 1982

Home Office Standing Advisory Committee on Police Dogs

Sir James Crane CBE, H M Chief Inspector of Constabulary (Chairman)

Sir Peter Matthews CVO OBE QPM DL, Chief Constable, Surrey Constabulary (Vice Chairman)

E J Boothby Esq, Chief Constable, Durham Constabulary

D Cree Esq, Commander, A 8 Branch, Metropolitan Police

G M Bird Esq, Assistant Chief Constable, Lothian & Borders Police

W H Gibson Esq, CBE QPM, Assistant Commissioner 'A' Department, Metropolitan Police

K Henshaw Esq, QPM, Chief Constable, North Yorkshire Police

Sir John Hermon, OBE, Chief Constable, Royal Ulster Constabulary

C H Kelly Esq, QPM LLB, Chief Constable, Staffordshire Police

A Laugharne Esq, QPM, Chief Constable, Lancashire Constabulary

C McLachlan Esq, QPM MA LLB, Chief Constable, Nottinghamshire Constabulary

B H Weight Esq, Chief Constable, Dorset Police

J Woodcock Esq, QPM, Chief Constable, South Wales Constabulary

Home Office Standing Advisory Committee on Police Dogs

Training Sub-Committee

Sir Peter Matthews CVO OBE QPM DL, Chief Constable, Surrey Constabulary (Chairman)

Chief Inspector J B Tyrrell, Durham Constabulary (Secretary)

Chief Inspector A Clarke, Metropolitan Police

Inspector H Edwards, Royal Ulster Constabulary

Chief Inspector B Eland, West Mercia Constabulary

Inspector J Gummery, South Wales Constabulary

Chief Inspector I Hoban, Lancashire Constabulary

Chief Inspector F Parsons, Strathclyde Police

Chief Inspector B Phillips, Staffordshire Police

Chief Superintendent D Trew, Metropolitan Police

Chief Inspector R Wood, Nottinghamshire Constabulary

Inspector S Wood, Surrey Constabulary

CONTENTS

Part I

Chapter 1

OBEDIENCE TRAINING

1 Complete control is the groundwork on which all succeeding training is based. The successful teaching of obedience is brought about by a series of repetitive habit forming exercises taught on command and put into practice under guidance with the latter being discontinued at the earliest possible moment. It is not to be expected that in teaching a dog a new exercise it will be immediately aware of what is to be done or how to associate a command with the required action. Before it does so, the same command, tone of voice and guided action will have to be carried out on numerous occasions. Care must be taken to avoid boredom to both dog and handler.

2 The various exercises which constitute general obedience are introduced in a certain progressive sequence which ultimately piece together. The dog must thoroughly grasp each exercise before progressing to another. It must be borne in mind that dogs, just as human beings, are diverse in character. Some are quicker in response to training, others are more sensitive and all have their off moments.

3 As training progresses the dog will learn to associate certain happenings with certain localities, sounds or people, and react accordingly. Whilst this type of association must be avoided at all costs in criminal work training, it is, conversely, the basis upon which rests the eventual standard of the obedience training. In this training the dog is expected to react in a set manner each time it hears or sees a specific command. To obtain this behaviour in a dog the commands, temperament and actions of the handler must always remain the same. Variations will only puzzle the dog and make training more difficult.

4 Words of command should be clear, concise and therefore preferably confined to single syllables. It is the sound and tone of the voice, not the volume, which controls the dog. The quieter the commands are given the better, as this will not only compel the dog to pay attention, but will help to build up its concentration. Commands must not be repeated as a bad association will be created in the dog's mind which will lead to faulty training. The dog, from the first day of training, must never be allowed to ignore a command or fail to complete one given. The dog must never be allowed to suspect that there is ever a *possibility* of being able to avoid a command. To allow one to be ignored for any reason whatsoever can give a dog a false impression, which, if allowed to develop, will make many problems in the ensuing training. It is for this reason that training in all exercises must be commenced when the dog is restrained on the lead and, therefore, can be guided instantly into the action required. At the commencement of training the word of command may be accompanied by physical influence and, in the intermediate stages, if necessary, by such visual aids as hand signals. Infinite patience is needed in showing the dog what it is required to do. Faults must be corrected at the time.

5   Disobedience must be met with firmness once it is certain that the dog has clearly understood the meaning of the command and has learnt the exercise correctly. The dog does not understand our standards of right and wrong and it is important, from the training point of view, that we do not wrongly credit it with these powers when considering the right application of correction. The use of physical punishment should only be resorted to in cases of emergency, and under no circumstances should it ever be considered a training measure. Proper use of the check chain, the verbal command or admonition and the withholding of praise are usually sufficient correctives. Care must also be taken that the habit of flicking the dog with the hands or lead is not allowed to develop. As shown above dogs are diverse in character and it is important that correction fits the temperament of the dog as well as the misdeed.

6   Nagging must be avoided at all times as must also boring or overtiring the dog by continuing the exercises too long.

7   Working happiness should prevail throughout the training by giving plenty of praise. This praise must be given even if the dog has had difficulty in doing its exercise but has completed it successfully. The manner and amount of such praise must of course vary with each dog but, having been praised suitably, the dog will know that it has done the right thing and the subsequent repetitive commands will be made much easier to enforce. A period of training should always finish on both a happy and successful note.

8   *Control in training does not only mean control over the dog. It is essential that the handler has control over himself. Any loss of temper, with the consequent aftermath of faulty training, will completely confuse the dog and make difficult the mutual understanding which is so essential between handler and dog.*

Obedience exercises

i) Heel on lead
Word of command: *'heel'*
The object of this exercise is to require the dog to walk readily and cheerfully on the left side of the handler with its right shoulder close to the handler's left knee. The lead should be held in a loop in the right hand. When the dog is correctly at heel, the lead should be slack. Should firm correction become necessary, it should be given by means of a jerk with the lead loosened immediately, as opposed to a pull.

Initially, the dog may resist being on the lead. This may be overcome by allowing the dog to trail it for short periods. It may also be necessary for the handler to allow himself to be led by the dog for short distances until the dog gets used to being on the lead. No attempt should be made to introduce the dog to this fundamental obedience exercise until he is thoroughly used to the lead.

Fondling with the left hand plays an important part in encouraging and praising the dog during this exercise. The dog should be given every opportunity to make mistakes and if caused mild discomfort when out of position, but praised by voice and hand when correct, it will soon learn the correct position it should occupy. Great care should, therefore, be taken to avoid any discomfort to the dog when in its correct position beside the handler.

Walking to heel on the lead should be practised with frequent variations of pace. As progress is made, right, left and about turns should be included. Any failure to comply with change of pace or direction should be corrected by a firm jerk of the lead. In the case of a lagging dog this fault should be overcome by the handler increasing his pace and encouraging the dog to *come* into the right position.

ii) Heel free
Word of Command: *'heel'*
This is a natural development of the previous exercise and its object is to instil in the dog the same constant positional sense as before, without the assistance of the lead. Success in this phase is entirely dependent on the standard achieved in i).

Training should be commenced from the 'sit' position (see para iv page 3). The lead may be carried across the shoulder. It should not be carried in such a way as to interfere with the handling or working of the dog. Furthermore, it must not be carried in a threatening manner or in any position where it can be used for this purpose. Early practice in this exercise should be limited to fairly straight walking with variations in pace introduced as progress is made. Turns to the left, right, and about turns should be incorporated as efficiency increases.

iii) Stand
Word of Command: *'stand'*
The object is to train the dog to remain in a stationary position as commanded.

This training should be given with the dog in the heel position whilst on the lead as in i), and should be practised by the handler gradually slowing down his pace of walking with the dog. The command 'stand' should be given and at the same time the handler will place his left hand gently in front of the dog's eyes so that its vision is obscured. The dog will then instinctively remain stationary. The handler will then place the lead on the ground, take a pace forward and face the dog. Any movement by the dog must be corrected by the command *'stand'*. After a brief period the handler will return to his dog, resume the correct 'heel on lead' position and continue with the exercise.

iv) Sit
Word of Command: *'sit'*
The object of this exercise is to teach the dog to take up a sitting position when commanded to do so by the handler. The dog must be introduced to this exercise whilst on the lead. The handler will adopt the stationary position with the dog at heel. Giving the command *'sit'*, he will simultaneously exert downward pressure on the hind quarters of the dog with his left hand. To prevent forward movement, upward pressure should

STAND SIT DOWN OFF LEAD

Stand

Sit

Down

3

Training for stand

Training for sit

Training for down

be applied with a shortened lead. The dog should then adopt a comfortable and balanced position with hind quarters and front legs in line. (See photograph 5.) Any deviation from this position, e.g. a crooked sit, should be corrected by exerting sufficient sideways pressure with the left hand towards the handler; or alternatively, straining the dog by applying slight sideways pressure with the left leg. After a brief period the handler will return to the correct 'heel on lead' position, take a step forward and complete the exercise.

v) Down
Word of Command: *'down'*

This exercise, which requires the dog to assume a recumbent position with all four legs touching the ground, is the essence of absolute control – a complete act of submission by the dog. The aim of this phase of training is to ensure that the dog will drop instantly on command or signal, even when at a distance from the handler.

Introduction to this exercise should be made when the dog is on the lead. Assistance and encouragement should be given by the handler applying gentle pressure with the left hand just behind the withers with a backward and downward movement. At the same time downward pressure will be applied by the right hand on the shortened lead. The command *'down'* should be given simultaneously with the pressure. When the dog takes up the correct position, both forms of pressure must be discontinued. Prolonged use of pressure will result in natural resistance which will defeat the purpose of the exercise. Should the dog make any attempt to rise, the pressures must be re-applied.

This exercise should be practised from all stationary positions as well as when the dog is walking to heel. As the dog fully understands the purport of the command, the use of pressure by the handler should be dispensed with.

vi) Introduction to distant control
Subsequent training for operational purposes will require the dog to work under control at a distance from its handler. It is therefore necessary to ensure that the appropriate obedience exercises described so far should be developed gradually to this end.

The first aim should be that the dog will remain in the correct position on command whilst the handler continues his forward direction. To achieve this, the handler should limit the distance travelled forward after giving the appropriate command to about 5 yards. He should then turn about, return to his dog by passing on the left side and coming from behind into the 'heel free' position. On the command *'heel'* both dog and handler will move forward. This should be practised from the 3 stationary positions but experience has shown that if confusion and indecision in the mind of the dog is to be avoided, the exercises should be carried out strictly in the sequence 'stand', 'sit' and 'down'.

It is important that once the dog understands what is required in this development, the exercises should not be practised too frequently to the detriment of 'heel free' working, e.g. by the dog anticipating commands and/or lagging behind the handler.

SIT AT HEEL

Front view

Side view

Rear view

DISTANCE CONTROL

Stand

Sit

Down

DISTANCE CONTROL HAND SIGNALS

Stand

Sit

Down

5

Having trained the dog to remain stationary in relatively remote positions, it is now necessary to train it to respond to specific commands and signals which may be given by its handler. This is an advancement on the above exercise and should be practised with the handler facing the dog.

In the early stages it may be necessary for the handler to train from the 'heel on lead' position but he should adopt the frontal position as soon as the dog is responding to his commands. As before, the distance at which this should be practised should not exceed approximately 5 yards until the dog fully understands the exercise. Thereafter, the distance may be progessively increased and hand signals as alternatives to oral commands introduced.

vii) Leaving the dog
Word of Command: *'stay'*

The object of this exercise is to ensure that the dog will remain in the 'down' position when so directed by the handler in circumstances when the handler finds it necessary to leave his dog for a period either within sight of or out of sight of the dog.

No attempt should be made to introduce this training until a satisfactory standard has been reached in the 'down' exercise described in para v) above and even then no attempt should be made to hurry the exercise. Experience has shown that it is far better to progress slowly with the dog remaining where directed for short periods at short distances from the handler rather than to attempt longer times and distances unsuccessfully.

From the outset of the training for this exercise, handlers should realise that *under no circumstances should the dog be recalled from the position in which it has been directed to stay.*

The exercise should be commenced with the dog in the 'down' position. After giving the command *'stay'* the handler will take up a position a short distance away but still within view of the dog. The handler should be alert to anticipate and check any movement. After a short interval the handler will return to his dog and take up the 'heel free' position. After a short pause he will give the command *'heel'*, take a step forward and complete the exercise.

As progress is made, the distance and time will be increased until eventually the dog will remain steady under all circumstances even with the handler out of sight.

If at any time during this exercise the dog moves out of position, the handler will return immediately and correct the fault by placing the dog in its original position.

viii) Recall
Word of Command: *'come'*

This is a most important obedience exercise in which the object is to secure on command the immediate return of the dog to the handler under all circumstances. The word of command should be given briskly with an urgency of purpose. An immediate response from the dog must be insisted upon at all stages of the training, although in no circumstances should the dog be punished for failing to return on command. It is most important that

6

Sit in front following recall

Lead being transferred right to left hand

Dog being directed round back of the handler

Being placed in sit at heel position

Finish position rear view

the dog should appreciate that whenever it returns to its handler, it is always very welcome.

The dog should be introduced initially to this exercise whilst walking to heel on the lead as in i). Whilst practising i) the handler should change direction away from the dog, at the same time calling and encouraging the dog to him, if necessary by gently drawing on the lead. Crouching and stepping backwards will give added encouragement to the dog. Every response from the dog should be praised.

This exercise should be practised from all the stationary positions in iii), iv), v), vi) and vii), but it is again emphasised that no attempt should be made to teach the dog the recall until it has completely mastered the stationary positions described above, in which it is clearly laid down that the handler should return to the dog.

The distances at which this exercise is practised should be progressively increased as in vii) and should eventually include recalling the dog in

7

Handler offering dumb-bell

circumstances where the handler is out of sight of the dog.

It is of the utmost importance in all stages of recall training that no hurt or discomfort is caused to the dog as it approaches or reaches the handler. The primary object of the exercise is the dog's complete obedience to the command '*come*'. Initially no more should be expected of the dog but as and when the dog can be relied upon to obey the command in a happy and lively manner, he should be trained to take up the 'sit' position as in iv) in front of the handler. When proficiency in this has been achieved, the exercise should be extended to include a final 'heel' position as in ii).

Extreme patience by the handler is required in all stages of this important exercise. In no circumstances should the dog be punished for failing to return on command.

RETRIEVE ON LEAD INITIAL STAGES OF TRAINING

Dumb-bell placed between jaws

Dog holding dumb-bell – handler praising

Dog holding dumb-bell at heel position

Dog holding dumb-bell frontal position

Dog carries dumb-bell towards handler

Delivery position

8

ix) Retrieve

Word of Command: *'fetch'*

The object of this most important exercise is to train the dog to fetch any retrievable object and return it undamaged to the handler. All handlers should realise that the exercise is the foundation on which a great deal of subsequent training depends and that it forms the basis of much of their practical police duty.

Experience has shown that in the initial stages of this exercise a wooden dumb-bell of appropriate size and weight to the type of dog being trained is the most suitable article to be retrieved and that the dog should be allowed to familiarise itself with the dumb-bell from the outset.

It is also necessary to ensure that the area used for training is free from any distractions which may interfere with the dog's concentration.

The exercise should be introduced in 3 definite stages as follows:

1   The hold

The exercise should commence with the dog on the lead in the 'sit at heel' position. The handler should hold the dumb-bell in his right hand and the lead in his left hand. The dog should be encouraged to take hold of the dumb-bell and when it responds should be definitely praised by stroking the top of its head. After a brief pause, the command *'leave'* should be given and the dumb-bell removed gently from the dog's mouth. Any reticence on the part of the dog to hold the dumb-bell or to reject it after it has been placed in its mouth should be overcome by the handler applying pressure with the left hand to the side of the dog's jaw whilst placing the dumb-bell in its mouth with the right hand. The lead in these circumstances should be looped over the left arm. When the dog is holding the dumb-bell, slight upward pressure to the underside of the dog's lower jaw should be applied. Oral praise in an encouraging manner should accompany the pressure. The command *'leave'* as above should be given and the dumb-bell removed gently from the dog's mouth.

Every opportunity should be taken to associate the dog's action in taking and maintaining hold of the dumb-bell with the command *'fetch'* and the taking of the dumb-bell from the dog with the command *'leave'*.

It is important that no form of pressure or correction should be administered whilst the dog is holding the dumb-bell.

2   The carry

When the dog is willingly taking the dumb-bell into its mouth on the command *'fetch'* and holding it firmly until the command *'leave'*, training to carry the article should commence by the handler positioning himself in front of the dog, still retaining the lead in his left hand in such a manner as to avoid any interference with the dumb-bell. The handler should then back slowly away from the dog, at the same time encouraging it to come to him. Any reluctance on the part of the dog to respond should be overcome by applying gentle pressure with the lead. Under no circumstances should this pressure be applied with a sudden jerk of the lead.

Should the dog have a tendency to drop the dumb-bell whilst moving forward, it should be replaced in the dog's mouth as in i) above. Oral correction should be administered in a tone which indicates displeasure.

Handler throwing dumb-bell

3 The delivery

As the dog understands what is required, the handler should 'halt' after a few backward steps from it and bring it into the 'sit in front' position. The command *'leave'* will be given after a brief pause and the dumb-bell gently removed from the dog's mouth.

Practice as above should be developed to a stage where the dog will pick up the dumb-bell from the ground on the command *'fetch'*, carry it a few paces and hold it until the command *'leave'*.

The use of the lead should then be dispensed with and the exercise practised with the handler throwing the dumb-bell a short distance and the dog retrieving it on command. The distance the dumb-bell is thrown should be progressively increased until a stage is reached where the dog from a steady 'heel free' position will move speedily in a direct line towards the dumb-bell on command, pick it up cleanly and deliberately return by the

RETRIEVE OFF LEAD

Approach

Pick-up

Carry

Approaching delivery position

Delivery

Finish

10

most direct route to its handler, take up the 'sit' position in front of him and on the command *'leave'* will allow the handler to remove it freely and then on command take up the 'heel free' position.

When this stage is reached, and not before, other suitable articles of varying size, shape and weight should replace the dumb-bell as the object of retrieve. Should the dog reject any alternative article, e.g. a metal article, the handler should return to the basic principles of familiarisation, pressure on the jaws and encouragement as in 1 and 2 above.

x) Speak (on command)
Word of Command: *'speak'*

Later training of dogs for police work will require the ability of the dog to bark in defined circumstances. Most dogs undergoing the obedience training dealt with so far will have found occasion to give voice of their own accord. The trainer must seize every occasion when the dog does speak to teach it to associate such action with the appropriate command.

xi) Send away
Word of Command: *'away'*

The object of this exercise is to train the dog to leave the handler and go in a prescribed direction or directions on command from the handler. This is a most difficult exercise and success in it cannot be achieved without even greater patience, determination and understanding on the part of the handler than is necessary for the previous exercises. It is important too that no attempt should be made to train for the 'send away' until the 'control at distance' has been mastered.

The exercise requires complete concentration by the dog.

The open area used for the initial training for 'send away' must be completely free from the activities of other dogs or any other distractions. A particular spot, preferably at the side of a hedge or fence in which there are no outstanding features such as a large tree or post should be selected. The handler, with the dog on the lead, should position himself about 5 yards distant facing that spot. He should bring the dog into the 'stand' position,

SEND AWAY (STRAIGHT)

Handler indicating direction

Dog being taken in direction

Dog in position

Handler returns to dog and gives praise

give the command 'away', take the dog forward to the selected spot and leave it there in the 'stand' position. The handler should return to his original starting position, pause for a short period and then return to the dog and praise it enthusiastically. These actions should be repeated so that the dog develops a confidence and strong happy association with the selected spot. Practice should continue until on the command 'away' the dog takes the initiative by displaying a willingness to take up the established position of its own accord. When this stage is reached, the use of the lead should be dispensed with and the distance between the handler and the selected spot progressively increased until it is possible to 'send away' in a direct line to a distance between 60 and 100 yards.

Training so far has been limited to one direction in a direct line. Before attempting to send the dog forward in another direction, a new area for training should be used so as to ensure that the proposed line of 'send away' does not encroach on ground previously used. It will still be necessary to use a particular objective such as a fence or hedge and the initial distance for such training must approximate to that first used for 'send away' training and increased progressively as the dog becomes competent.

If for any reason the dog does not respond satisfactorily in the changed surroundings, the handler should resume practice in the original area.

When the dog has mastered the exercise, the 'recall' may be introduced but if it shows any unsteadiness or tendency to anticipate recall, correction should be given. The handler should then collect the dog as distinct from recalling it.

xii) Re-direction with extended arm signals

The object of this exercise is to train the dog to go in a specified direction on command when working at a distance from the handler.

It is of the utmost importance that, in the initial stages of re-direction training, no attempt should be made to carry it out in conjunction with

SEND AWAY (RE-DIRECTION)

Dog in position

Handler moving right sideways re-directs dog

12

'send away' training. Any such action taken too early would only confuse the dog to the detriment of both exercises.

Once again, the area for this training must be selected as for the 'send away' training.

Training will commence with the handler leaving his dog in the 'stand' position and facing it from a distance of approximately 10 yards. He should fully extend his right arm sideways, give the command *'right'* and move in that direction, at the same time encouraging the dog to respond accordingly. Initially the handler should move to the right for only a short distance. After giving the command *'stay'*, he will go to the dog and give encouraging praise. The dog should normally respond quickly to this training and as it does the distance involved should be progressively increased. As direction to the right is mastered similar training for direction to the left should be introduced.

Handler goes to dog and gives praise

When a stage has been reached where the dog responds to signals to the right and to the left up to about 25 yards, the handler should gradually, at the commencement of the exercise, increase the distance between himself and the dog. The recall may also be introduced.

When satisfied that the dog will respond satisfactorily at about 100 yards distance in the familiar setting, new areas for training may be introduced. If there is any deterioration in the dog's response in a strange area, the training should be resumed in the original setting.

Training should continue on the above lines until a stage is reached where the handler with the dog in the 'heel free' position is capable of sending it in any specific direction until it reaches a required distance. On the command *'stay'*, the dog should remain in the 'stand' position there and after a pause should respond to the direction to the left or to the right and again remain standing where directed on the command *'stay'*. When recalled the dog should return to the handler at a fast pace by the most direct route.

The handler should be able to halt the dog during recall but this should not be overdone as the dog will become apprehensive and may anticipate such a command to the detriment of a speedy recall. Immediate return on command to the handler is essential under all conditions. Nothing should be introduced to this part of training which may mitigate against such immediate response by the dog.

xiii) Agility

All dogs considered for police work must be agile in their own right before selection. The agility phase of training in these fundamental obedience exercises is calculated to ensure the maximum use of this natural agility. It is therefore necessary to emphasise that all the exercises shown below are essentially a development of obedience training.

The object of agility training is to ensure that the police dog learns how to surmount all obstacles within its physical capabilities on command, and under control. It is important that this training should be limited to the known capabilities of the breed. Any attempt to over-reach in this direction may well be disastrous to the dog's physique and mental approach.

a) Jumping
Word of Command: *'up'*

The dog should be introduced to this phase of training by being required to jump low obstacles which can be surmounted without difficulty by the handler. Initially, the training should be carried out with the dog on the lead but the handler should exercise care that the lead does not check or impede the dog's natural jumping movement.

3FT CLEAR JUMP

Taking up position

Take off

Clearance

Care must also be taken to ensure the dog approaches the middle of the obstacle to avoid any tendency to try to circumvent it. There is no hard and fast rule as to the distance from the obstacle at which the dog should make its jump, but the handler by observation should time the word of command to coincide with the take-off.

As soon as the dog understands the purport of the exercise and the word of command, it must be required to take up a stationary position on landing. Ability to do this is a fundamental element of control. Training over comparatively low obstacles should be continued until the dog is proficient in controlled jumping of this nature. The use of the lead and the practice of the handler surmounting the obstacle with the dog should be dispensed with as soon as the dog fully understands the training. Obstacles may increase in height as and when the dog displays the necessary aptitude. It is essential in this phase of training that the dog should clear the obstacle and that this training is not confused with later agility exercises.

b) Scramble-Board for scaling high obstacles
Word of Command: 'over'

The object of this training is to teach the dog to negotiate obstacles which are too high for it to jump and which may only be overcome by the dog leaping upwards and pulling itself over. As in the previous exercise there is no set distance at which the dog should commence its leap upwards, but generally it should be positioned at a distance equal to the height to be reached.

14

Handler and dog take up position   **Dog scaling**   **Dog overcomes obstacle**

The exercise should be commenced with comparatively low suitable obstacles and practised with gradual increases in height as progress is made. As with jumping, great care is necessary to ensure the dog is never required to exceed its physical capabilities. There is an additional hazard in this phase in that too much landing on hard ground or from too great a height is to be avoided.

As and when the dog is proficient in scaling, the obedience requirement to remain in a stationary position after landing should be enforced. The exercise should be extended to include returning over the obstacle on command. Subsequently, practice and training in retrieving (see ix), involving a return over the obstacle may be introduced.

Recommended construction of scramble-board – see page 66

Dog prepares to land

c) Long jumping

Word of Command: *'up'* or *'over'*

The above agility exercises have been confined to surmounting obstacles of some height. The ability to overcome obstacles of width is a normal development of the previous training. As with jumping under a), the dog should be introduced to this exercise by being required to negotiate suitably low obstacles placed quite close together. With practice the dog should quickly appreciate the difference in this type of jump; the distance between the obstacles should be progressively increased. It is essential that all long jump training should be continued within the physical capabilities of the dog as in a) and b) overleaf.

INITIAL TRAINING ON LEAD

LONG JUMP

ADVANCED TRAINING OFF LEAD

xiv) Water work

The fully trained police dog must obviously be capable of crossing water obstacles. Whereas many dogs take naturally to water, others have to be trained to it. Any diffidence to entering water must be overcome by progessive training. Training of such dogs should commence near a smooth stretch of water with a gently sloping bed. Initially the dog should be encouraged to walk around in the shallow water. In some circumstances it may be advisable for the handler to enter the water with the dog to build up the necessary confidence. Whilst in the water the dog should be encouraged to retrieve suitable floating objects thrown by the handler. Careful development of this training by gradually increasing the distance and the depth of the water to which the object is thrown, will usually result in the dog swimming where appropriate without difficulty.

Training in water work should be limited to suitable times of the year.

16

xv) Gunfire

In order to assess the potentialities of a trainee dog in relation to gunfire, and to ensure the dog possesses the necessary qualifications for later training in criminal work, it is necessary, at an early stage, that its reaction to gunfire should be tested. The introduction to gunfire must be careful and gradual; faulty training may well ruin a promising dog.

Gunfire should not be made an issue; during the course of other training exercises whilst the dog is on the lead, the instructor, at a distance of not less than 100 yards and out of sight should fire a .22 weapon occasionally. The reaction of the dog should be closely observed and if any signs of nervousness are shown the dog should be rejected.

Chapter 2

SCENT

1   The dog, like most animals, in its wild state depended to a large extent on its nose for survival and it is a scientific fact that a dog has a sense of smell immeasurably keener than that of a human being. Use of this characteristic is the means by which a dog is able, under certain conditions, to follow a trail.

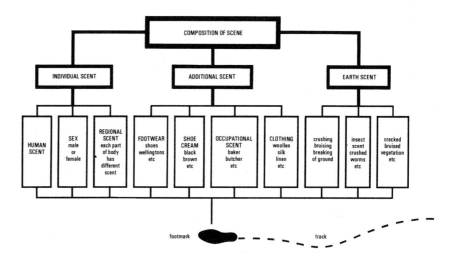

2   The theory of scent is a wide and complex subject but for practical police purposes may be divided into broad categories as follows:
   i) Ground scent; and
   ii) Wind scent.

Ground Scent

3   Ground scent, which is followed by the dog in tracking, is caused by contact with the ground resulting in disturbance. The slightest movement of the soil or the crushing of grass, other vegetation and insect life, leaves particles and/or drops of moisture lying on the ground, all of which give off a scent and thus denote a trail. Some of this scent will obviously adhere to the crushing instrument, e.g. the footwear, and may be carried in this way for some distance from one type of ground to another. Experience has shown that the dog depends to a large extent on this effect from crushing in following a track.

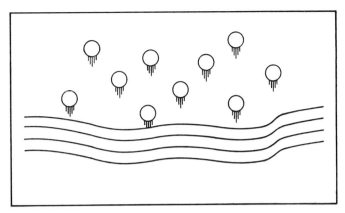

Footprint on soil.

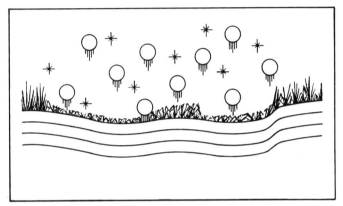

Footprint on soil and grass.

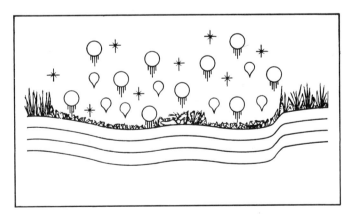

Footprint on soil and grass and the insects therein.

Gaseous odours rising.

Crushed insect odours.

Crushed grass odours.

Wind borne scent

4 Wind scent is the name given to the scent which attracts the dog in searching. It is air borne from the individual or object and may, in the former case, be described as the personal odour from the body of the person concerned; in the latter it may be characteristic to the object or may be the result of some previous human contact. The scent of the article itself may be alien to the particular ground on which it lies, e.g. a piece of sawn or broken wood lying on grassland. The amount of personal odour varies according to constitution, health, clothing, nourishment, activity, mental condition and state of cleanliness. It is greatly intensified when there is physical exertion.

5 Wind scent may also include occupational odours carried in the clothing of the wearer. In some circumstances they may be very characteristic and distinctive.

6 The dog using its acute sense of smell becomes conscious of the scent through the air it breathes. The degree of discernment therefore varies with the concentration of the scent which in turn varies with the rate of evaporation, air movement and type of country over which the scent is set up. Quite obviously the most important feature affecting scent from an operational point of view is time. The more quickly a dog can be brought to follow a scent the more successful the result is likely to be.

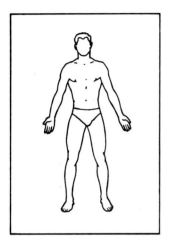

Natural body odours.

Components of footwear which affect the composition of the tracking scent.

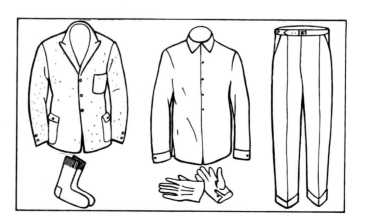

The natural scent is changed by the type and nature of clothing and occupation of the wearer (i.e. Harris Tweed as against Serge Suit).

20

Factors affecting scent

7 Scent is subject to evaporation and is therefore greatly affected by climatic conditions. Generally speaking scenting conditions are most favourable:

    i) in mild, dull weather;

    ii) when the temperature of the ground is higher than the air, i.e., normally at night time;

    iii) in areas where the ground is sheltered.

8 Factors which adversely affect scent are:

    i) hot sunshine;

    ii) strong winds;

    iii) heavy rainfall after the scent has been set up.

9 Frost and snow may have either the effect of preserving or destroying a scent depending on whether this occurs before or after the scent has been occasioned.

10 Pedestrian or vehicular traffic will quickly disperse a scent.

11 The foregoing, already described as a wide and complex subject, is one which must be interpreted with great care when working a dog under practical conditions. There will be innumerable occasions when the accepted theories are contradicted by the dog's ability and willingness to follow a scent which under accepted conditions should be non-existent. The only true test is for the dog to be given the opportunity to establish whether or not working conditions prevail.

Chapter 3

TRACK LAYING AND TRACKING

Track laying

1 Before any attempt is made to teach a dog to track, it is essential that anyone concerned in training, i.e. dog handlers, track layers and instructors, should realize the importance of the manner in which the dog is introduced to this form of training.

2 The progress of the dog in the tracking exercises depends entirely on the understanding, care and planning which is necessary if a high standard of efficiency is to be achieved.

3 Each track, at every stage of the training, should be carefully planned so that the possibility of the dog experiencing failure is reduced to the minimum.

4 The following rules should be adhered to:
  i Lay a track which is appropriate to the stage of training.
  ii Ensure that the start of the track is easily identified. If necessary a marker may be used for this purpose.
  iii Remember the precise route taken from the start. If necessary landmarks or natural immovable objects can be used for this purpose.
  iv Turns and changes of direction must be carefully planned and pinpointed.
  v Wind direction should always be taken into account so that no interference is caused by incorrectly placed articles or other sections of the track.
  vi Ensure that articles are placed carefully on the track and not dropped carelessly downwind.
  vii Always make certain that a large article is placed at the end of the track so that successful completion is assured.
  viii To avoid any danger of the dog wind scenting the end of the track and article, or the possibility of it inadvertently wandering onto the last part of the track, there should be a substantial distance between the start and finish.
  ix The practice of following the side of fences, hedges and walls should be avoided so that the dog does not develop an undesirable habit of being attracted to and consequently following these lines.
  x The track layer should always ensure that he is not compelled to retrace his steps by careless planning of the track.

Cross track

5 The making of a cross track must be painstaking in order to avoid confusion. The person laying the track must have the assistance of a second person and must explain to him in detail the course of the main track.

6 The early cross tracks should always be laid at right angles to the main track and must be at a point where the main track is running straight. Failure to do this will lead to confusion by the dog.

7 The handler must carefully watch both the main track and cross track being laid in order to be fully aware of their location.

Tracking

8 The object of this aspect of training is to teach the dog to follow by scent a selected trail so that the dog is eventually capable of following a specific scent to the exclusion of other distractions and, at the same time, of indicating to the handler any item of property left on or adjacent to the track.

9 Training in tracking calls for extreme concentration on the part of both dog and handler. As far as the dog is concerned, it is essential that he must be fresh and alert and not in a tired condition. He must not be suffering from depression due to any recent failings in another phase of training. It is equally important that the handler should realise that this part of training calls for his full concentration and patience, and he must be at pains to ensure that he uses the same commands, intonations and actions in respect of tracking so that the dog will connect them with the job he has to do.

10 The importance of retrieving (see Chapter 1) will be emphasised during the training in tracking and progress in the latter depends especially in the early stages, on the ability and keenness of the dog in retrieving.

11 In considering the commands to be used for this phase of training the importance of the modulation of voice in giving the command *'seek'* must be appreciated. The command must not be given sharply or harshly, but rather in a quiet, coaxing manner with the command well drawn out. This will have the effect of consoling the dog, so that he may bring his full powers of concentration into action to learn to follow a particular line of scent to the exclusion of any other scents which might be present. To do this the dog must be taught to follow the line thoroughly from the beginning. The speed at which he follows it depends on the individual dog; some even at the start of this training prefer to move at a fairly quick pace, whilst others prefer a slower pace. It is the duty of the handler to note these highly important pointers. The track must be followed thoroughly and care must be taken to prevent him wandering. It is important that encouragement is given in the elementary stages of this training and even though some dogs will want to move at a fairly quick pace it should be steadied to the pace of the handler. This does not mean that the dog should be pulled back as this will tend to dishearten the dog.

12 The dog that is moving at a slower pace has to be encouraged gently and not boisterously. This type of dog should not be hurried.

13 The ground, preferably grassland, on which the first stages of training are to be carried out, should be free of other persons and animals.

14 The tracking harness (see Chapter 12, Part 3 on Equipment) should be worn by the dog for this training and experience has confirmed that the tracking harness with the extended training lead attached in lieu of the tracking line is more adaptable in the early stages. It is important that the dog should be introduced to and made familiar with the tracking harness some time before he is required to wear it in training. Failure to do this will result in much of the dog's concentration being lost whilst he is getting used to this equipment. New stiff harnesses should be avoided when possible; new leather should be suitably treated with leather oil before the dog is required to wear it. Once he has got used to it, it must only be used for tracking. The wearing of it indicates to the dog that he has got to concentrate on tracking.

Reading the dog on track

15 Knowledge of the exact position of the track in the early stages of training will enable the handler to observe the behaviour of the dog as the track is being followed. The reactions of different dogs when following a track vary considerably and it is the duty of every dog handler to understand clearly at the outset of training in tracking the individual reactions of his dog. In particular the handler should be observant to note and appreciate the reactions of the dog when wandering from the known track and the reactions when the dog re-discovers it. The position of the head, the manner in which the tail is carried, dropped or moved should be noted in relation to the accuracy with which the dog is following the set track. With practice and intelligent observation the handler should become familiar with the reactions of the dog, knowledge of which is invaluable when, at a later stage, the dog is required to track on strange scents on a track which is also unknown to the handler. Failure in practical tracking is more often than not due to a handler who thinks he knows more than the dog. Only the complete understanding of the dog's reactions at all times will enable this to be reduced to a minimum.

TRACK

Dog on training lead left in 'down' position

Aids to instruction in tracking

16 In the early stages of training, it is necessary to place at the end of the track to encourage the dog to retrieve it, an object with which the dog is familiar and in which it displays a keen interest. It should not be forgotten that this object, which is to be used as a reward, is the last object which is to be placed on the track when the dog advances to more than one article being used. It is the articles in between the commencement and end of the track that develop the power of concentration in the dog.

17 There should be no limit to the type and material of objects used, except that any which may be injurious to the dog's mouth must be avoided. The dog should be familiar with all such objects by having retrieved them, before they are used in the more elementary tracking training.

Tracking: first stage

18 This stage of tracking is limited to training the dog to follow a straight track which has been laid within sight of the dog. It is the foundation for all further training in tracking and should be completely mastered before any variations or additions are introduced.

Handler prepares dog for tracking

Handler indicates start of track

Dog commences tracking

19 The handler with his dog on the lead should stand so that he can see the actions of the track layer.

20 The track layer should produce an article with which the dog is familiar. The dog must be encouraged to renew its interest in the article. The track layer will lay a straight track of approximately 30 yards. After making sure that the dog has seen his action, he will place the article on the ground at his feet. He will return to the start of the track by a semi-circular route which must be down wind of the track.

21 The dog must then be brought on the lead without delay to the start of the track. The tracking harness and extended training lead will be fitted. The handler should then give the command *'seek'* and encourage the dog to follow the line of the track. With the excitement generated by the track layer walking away with the article, most dogs will be extremely keen to reach the end of the track. When a dog shows reluctance encouragement should be used. When the dog finds the article the handler should give enthusiastic praise. He should remove the harness and then encourage the dog to get enjoyment from the article. This exercise should be repeated on similar new tracks.

On track

Side view on track

22 Training in this exercise will be discontinued if the dog shows any sign of fatigue or lack of interest.

23 As progress is made the length of the track should be gradually increased but still in a straight line. As the distance is increased and the dog becomes more confident and determined, the use of the lead will be discontinued and extended lead will be replaced by the tracking line. This will allow the dog to work at a greater distance from the handler, reduce his interference to the dog and ensure improved concentration.

Tracking: second stage

24 In the second stage of training in tracking the dog and handler will be introduced to tracks which have been laid out of view of the dog and will incorporate gradual increases in the length of the tracks laid. The time lag between the laying of the track and the introduction of the dog to the start of the track will be progressively increased.

25 The track layer will lay a track approximately 100 yards long in a straight line out of view of the dog. He will still establish a heavy scent pattern at the start of the track and will set off walking with shortened paces but, before completing the full distance, will assume a normal walking pace. He will again leave the familiar article at the end of the track.

26 The handler and the dog will still be brought to the start of the track without delay. It may be found that with the track having been laid out of sight the dog may display less enthusiasm for tracking but should quickly respond to encouragement from the handler.

27 At this stage it is important that a correct tracking technique be established. The instructor should ensure that the dog is tracking at an appropriate speed to its nature. Its nose should be close to the ground and it should display full concentration regardless of distractions. This aspect should take priority over increase in the length of tracks or the time lag between bringing the dog to the start of the track. At this stage of training it is helpful to the dog that the straight line track be laid in the same direction as the wind. This assists the dog in keeping its nose to the ground thereby concentrating on ground scent.

28 When the instructor is satisfied with the dog's working of the straight track, turns, which initially should all be at right angles, may be introduced. The distance between the turns should be approximately 50 yards. The time lag in introducing the dog to the start of the track is of little importance until the dog is consistently working tracks of approximately 300 yards laid out of sight and is correctly negotiating left and right turns without difficulty or overshooting.

29 It is imperative that throughout training in tracking the handler should appreciate the value of the track article. It is emphasized that the maximum amount of praise and enjoyment should accompany the finding of it.

Hard surface

30 While engaged on operational duties handlers will be called upon to work their dogs on hard surface tracks. These surfaces may vary from

Approaching the article

Indication of the article

Dog down by article

Handler recovering article

concrete to packed earth and may be traversed during the course of a track which may have commenced on any type of surface. Dogs can be trained to do this to a very high standard of proficiency provided that, in the early stages, the handler/ instructor *concentrates entirely on one type of surface until a satisfactory standard has been achieved.*

31 It cannot be over-emphasised that careful handling and encouragement will certainly be necessary if the dog is to become efficient and reliable in this work.

32 When the *instructor* is of the opinion that the dog displays a satisfactory standard of tracking ability he can then introduce it to hard surface tracking. It is important that initially he selects a suitable area where the hard surface is sufficiently broken so that there will be some degree of disturbance. Care should be taken in respect of the direction and strength of the wind. In the first instance only a very short track (30 yards), *all of which must be on hard surface*, should be attempted. It should be laid in a straight line with a suitable small article placed at the end. Because of the increased difficulties involved in this type of tracking the dog should be allowed to work the track immediately after it has been laid.

33 By following the principles outlined in the initial stages of tracking, distance and time can be gradually increased together with the inclusion of variations of surface. Eventually it will be possible to introduce the dog to tracks on pavements and roads in built up areas where there are distractions from pedestrian and vehicular traffic. When the dog has reached this standard of efficiency in hard surface tracking, *then and only then*, should the tracks be laid from one type of surface to another. These should include all types of surface, provided that the handler fully appreciates and recognises the changes indicated by the dog when working from one surface to another.

Line handling

34 As the dog improves at tracking, the tracking line will replace the extended lead. The handler should appreciate the importance of correct line handling.

35 The tracking line is not just the means of keeping in contact with the dog whilst it is working – it is a line of communication which, if properly used, will make the handler sensitive to the dog's movements and indications. The handler must also appreciate that the standard of his line handling has a strong influence on the efficiency eventually reached by his dog.

36 At the start of a track when the tracking line has been taken into use, the handler will carefully lay the line out on the ground to its full extent ensuring that it is free from knots and not tangled. After attaching the line to the harness, the handler will remove the lead, put it across his shoulders so that it does not interfere with his line handling, and then fit the harness to the dog. As the dog is set to work, the handler will gradually allow the line to pass through his hand until an appropriate distance between him and the dog has been reached. He must always ensure that he has not less than 6 feet of tracking line in reserve.

37 If the area over which the dog is working is overgrown, the distance between the dog and the handler must be such as to avoid interference with the line. The line should never be allowed to drop below the level of the dog's back and as far as possible should be kept in line along it. This should ensure that the tension of the line is consistent and applied so as not to interfere with the dog's concentration. When the dog changes direction whilst on the track, the handler will adjust the angle of the line accordingly. The handler must remain stationary until the dog has positively indicated the direction of the track.

Tracking: third stage

38 In this stage of training the dog will be required to track over a variety of terrains and surfaces, to give positive identification of finding articles on the track and the number of articles laid will be progressively increased and varied. In addition, the time lag between the laying and working of the tracks will be increased but great care must be taken to ensure that conditions are good.

39 It must be thoroughly understood that progess in this stage of training may be very slow. If for any reason the dog should experience difficulty in completing what to it is a more complicated track, its confidence must be immediately restored by working a fresh track which it is capable of completing successfully.

40 All tracks up to this stage of training have been completed by the dog working to the same familiar article. In future, by a gradual process, this familiar article will be replaced by a variety of other objects varying in size, shape and material.

41 Initially, the familiar article will be replaced by an article of similar size but of different material. The track layer, whilst laying the first few tracks, should take the strange article and the familar one with him. On reaching the end of the track he will place the strange article on the track, walk a further 10 to 15 paces and drop the familiar article.

42 When the dog completes a track and indicates the strange article, it should be placed in the 'down' position (Chapter 1 v)) without delay. The handler will drop the tracking line to the ground and *walk* up to his dog. The dog should remain in the 'down' position for a short time and the handler should give praise and engender the dog's interest in this new article. After a short time, he will remove the harness and encourage the dog to continue forward of its own accord until it finds the familiar article. The handler should repeat the phase associated with this article.

43 When the dog is going 'down' of its own accord after finding the strange article, the use of the familiar article can be dispensed with. It should, however, be permanently retained by the handler for end-of-track relaxation and praise when the harness has been removed from the dog.

44 In the early stages, certain dogs may display an inability to concentrate for lengthy periods. In these cases it will be of assistance if an additional article is placed approximately half way along the track. In these circumstances, the handler will take possession of this article when located and will require the dog to continue tracking until it reaches the final article. Ultimately, at this stage, the dog should be capable of working tracks up to one hour old, but handlers should not be unduly concerned if a dog is a little slow at reaching this standard provided it is making consistent progress.

45 All training in tracking to date has been limited to working in prepared conditions. In this stage of training it is necessary to train the dog and the handler to work under conditions which are likely to be met in the performance of active police duty. So far, although experience has been gained in tracking on different types of surface, it has been limited in any one track to one type of surface. In police duty it is, of course, most unlikely that any track to be followed will be limited to one type of surface. In order to fit the dog and handler for their effective role in police duty, all tracks in this stage of training should commence from simulated scenes of crime, e.g. buildings, roadways, etc., at which the handler will be called upon to use his powers of observation as a police officer and make a thorough examination of the scene before setting his dog to work.

46 These tracks should be very carefully planned so that the dog will gain experience in not only tracking over changes of surfaces but of overcoming a variety of obstacles likely to be encountered in practical police work and in retrieving a variety of types of articles abandoned on or near the track.

47 These changes should be introduced gradually and the handler must understand that continual failures would soon lead to despondency in the dog. In the event of failure, the instructor must ensure that the confidence of the dog and the handler is restored quickly by giving the opportunity to work a more simple track in a different area.

48 Operationally, it is of the utmost importance that the handler will be able to observe the actions of his dog on indicating articles. Although dogs vary in their indication they will generally go 'down' by the side of the article.

49 During this phase of instruction, dog handlers should be made to appreciate the value of including night training. This will normally improve a dog's tracking ability. In practice, when called to deal with a practical incident, it can be expected that there has been a certain amount of interference and fouling of any track which may have been left. It is therefore necessary in this final stage of training to include the laying of cross tracks. To avoid unnecessary confusion, the handler, track layer and the instructor should be fully aware of the exact location of any planned cross track. If for any reason the dog becomes interested in or strays on to cross tracks, correction sufficient to overcome the fault, but not such as to affect the dog's enthusiasm, should be given.

50 The direction and timing of cross tracks or other forms of interference must be adjusted methodically as training progresses until a stage is reached where the dog will completely ignore all forms of interference or fouling.

Chapter 4

SEARCHING

SEARCH FOR PROPERTY

Dog searching area

Searching
1 The object of teaching the dog to search is to ensure that it has the ability to retrieve property or give indication of property too large or too heavy to retrieve, to quarter and search buildings and open spaces for criminals or missing persons. It is completely separate and distinct from tracking and must not under any circumstances be confused with tracking either by the handler or the dog.

Search for property
2 Word of Command: *'fetch'*
The dog relies on finding property by means of air-borne scent and therefore should be trained to make full use of its scenting powers rather than its sight.
3 The success of all searching exercises depends to a great extent on the ability of the handler to observe and interpret the indications given by the dog in tracing an air-borne scent.

Indicates article

Pick up

Delivery

4 Handlers should pay particular attention accordingly.
5 The dog should have reached a fairly good standard in the 'retrieve' exercise (see Chapter 1, para 8) before being introduced to searching for property.

6 In the initial stages the articles used should be those with which the dog is familiar.

7 It is very important that the dog should be trained to be a keen and vigorous searcher. With this in mind the handler should never prolong the exercise until the dog becomes tired of searching and retrieving, and throughout the whole of the search for property the handler must never lose sight of the importance of the necessary praise and activity that should accompany the successful conclusion of the exercise.

8 In the early stages of searching for property in locations not known to the dog, it may be found that the dog may run off in its enthusiasm to find the article. With practice, and encouragement from the handler, it will soon steady down and show interest in the search.

9 In selecting suitable locations for placing the article, advantage should be taken of the direction of the wind. Whenever possible, the dog should be worked into the wind. This training should be commenced in the open air and at the outset one article only should be used. The handler, in full view of the dog, will place the article in a selected area which has sufficient growth to conceal it, making it necessary for the dog to use its nose to locate it. The handler will return to the dog and on the command '*fetch*' will release it. This should be repeated until the dog is searching successfully. As progress is made the dog should not witness the placing of the article.

10 As progress is made the venues, still in the open, for this training should be changed and additional articles introduced. The exercise should be repeated until the dog is capable of recovering a variety of articles.

Buildings

11 When searching for articles in the open has been mastered, exercises in buildings should be introduced. At first one article only should be thrown a short distance inside the building, distances being progressively increased. Eventually the handler will walk inside the building and place 2 or 3 articles in various positions (not always on the floor) and then by giving the command '*fetch*' require the dog to search for the articles.

12 The ultimate aim of this training in searching for articles suitably placed is to make the dog proficient in searching an unknown area of ground or building, to detect and, if possible, retrieve articles which may be alien to the surroundings and which may bear a scent. Operationally, such a search should be systematic in control in order to ensure that the whole area has been covered.

Search for irretrievable objects

Word of Command: '*fetch*'

13 Operationally, a dog may be searching for and may find property which is too bulky or heavy for it to retrieve. It is therefore necessary that the dog is trained to this contingency.

14 The handler, using a suitable article with which the dog is familiar, should throw it for the dog to retrieve. When the dog has made a determined attempt to retrieve it without success, the handler should give encouragement until the dog responds by barking. To achieve this object, repetition of the exercise will be necessary and it may be of assistance if the

Indication

Attempt to retrieve

Indication by barking

article is placed in some high position out of the dog's reach, within its view, e.g. on a tree, high fence, ledge, etc. When the dog attempts to reach the article it should be given encouragement until it responds by barking. When this happens, the handler should go quickly to the dog, recover the article and give enthusiastic praise. The dog should be given the opportunity of associating the article with the barking and praise. Repetition of this training will let the dog know that when he barks the handler will respond by getting the article.

15 When the dog has mastered this part of the exercise, the training should be continued but with the placing of the article out of view.

16 It is essential that training should be continued until the dog is efficient at finding and indicating the presence of an irretrievable article while working out of sight of his handler such as in thick undergrowth or during the hours of darkness.

17 The importance of the dog giving a determined and positive indication must be appreciated by the handler.

Search for persons

18 Word of Command: *'find him'*

The ability of the dog to search for persons, not necessarily criminals, in open areas as distinct from buildings, is of prime importance in practical police duty. This must be appreciated by all dog handlers.

19 In this stage of training 2 instructors, one of whom will adopt the role of 'criminal', should be employed. At the outset the ground used should be completely different from that on which training for tracking has been practised and, if possible, should consist of thick undergrowth or woodland, and be quite extensive.

20 The 'criminal' will select a suitable hiding place which will be known to the handler but not to the dog. The handler with his dog on the lead will walk down wind of the concealed 'criminal' at a few yards distance from him. Immediately the dog indicates that it is aware of the presence of the 'criminal', the handler will encourage it and give the command *'find him'*. The dog will be restrained on the lead until it gives a positive indication by barking. The dog should then be praised. Should the dog fail to bark following its initial indication of the presence of the 'criminal', it must be encouraged to do so by the command *'speak'*. (See Chapter 1, para 8x)).

21 The handler will then direct the 'criminal' to leave his place of hiding. The 'criminal' will then be treated as a suspected person, searched and escorted from the area. The dog will be positioned approximately 6 feet from the 'criminal' during searching and will keep him under surveillance.

22 This training will be repeated with a gradual increase of distance between the dog and the place of concealment until the dog is indicating the presence of the 'criminal' correctly and barking spontaneously. At this stage of training, the dog will be released from the lead at the point of indication. Under no circumstances must the dog be encouraged to do anything other than bark.

23 This training must be made as operationally realistic as possible. Although on occasion the 'criminal' may conceal himself clear of the ground, this should not be practised too frequently as this may encourage the dog to use its sight instead of its sense of smell.

Indicating by wind scent

Barking and containing

SEARCH (PERSONS) OPEN

Handler calls suspect to him

Suspect searched

Quartering

24 Training so far has been limited to the dog being on the lead until indication of the presence of the 'criminal'. As the distances in the foregoing exercise are increased, it will be necessary to conduct the search with the dog off the lead in a systematic manner in order to ensure that all the ground has been thoroughly searched. This method is known as 'quartering the ground' and should be introduced into the training as soon as the progress of the dog in searching and the increases in distance make it expedient to do so.

25 In order to ensure that the ground is completely covered, the handler should work his dog on command up to distances of 50 yards to the left and to the right in open country. In thick undergrowth or woodland, the distances to the right or left of the handler have to be considerably reduced. As the area to each side of the handler is covered, he should move forward slowly still directing his dog until the dog locates the air-borne scent from the 'criminal'.

26 In the initial stages, the 'criminal' should take up his place of concealment approximately 50 yards to the right or left of a pre-determined route which will be taken by the handler with his dog heel free. The 'criminal' should take up his place of concealment from outside the area in order to avoid any ground scent. The handler should then patrol along the pre-determined route and encourage his dog with the command *'find him'*. On locating the 'criminal', the dog should start barking. If it fails to do so, it should be excited by the 'criminal' and encouraged by the handler. When the dog is barking freely, the handler should approach the 'criminal' and after interrogation and search will complete the exercise by escorting the 'criminal' from the area.

27 This should be repeated with the 'criminal' concealing himself on the opposite side of the pre-determined route and subsequently alternating from one side to the other. The handler must be certain that the dog has searched the farthest point of the area before it is directed to a fresh area.

28 For operational purposes, when the dog is quite proficient in finding the hidden 'criminal', opportunity should be taken for the dog to conduct a search for property in the immediate area previously occupied by the 'criminal'. This should be done after the 'criminal' has been searched.

Search for persons – buildings

29 Although the dog has been trained to search for property in buildings in conjunction with the previous exercise, it must be appreciated that the search of buildings differs from the search elsewhere in that the air-borne scent may circulate in an erratic manner which may result in the dog giving an indication some distance from the actual place of concealment. This is due to the fact that a draught or artificial ventilation may have caused a concentration of scent elsewhere in the room than the place of concealment. This must be fully appreciated by the handler and the indication given by the dog accepted as positive evidence of someone present in the room etc. The handler will then thoroughly investigate as a policeman.

30 At first a building with several rooms should be used. The 'criminal' will take up a position in a room, known to the handler but out of direct

SEARCH (PERSONS) BUILDING

Dog searching building

Location and barking

Handler interrogation

view of the dog. The handler will remove the lead from the dog and give the command *'find'*. The dog will be directed to search one or two rooms before reaching the one known to be occupied by the 'criminal'. When the dog finds the 'criminal' and indicates this by barking, the procedure of interrogation, search and escort will be followed.

31 As progess is made in searching in buildings, the training can include circumstances where the 'criminal' is concealed from view in a cupboard or other convenient place. Initially, the door of the selected hiding place should be left slightly ajar, to assist the dog.

Operational searches

32 *Searches under operational conditions may well expose the dog to unseen permanent hazards and dangers not created by the criminal, e.g. machinery, exposed electric power, lift shafts, corrosive liquid containers, etc.*

Dogs should never be worked freely where any such danger may be anticipated by the handler. If in any doubt use the lead.

Chapter 5

CRIMINAL WORK

PROTECTIVE CANVAS

Instructor prepares to protect right forearm

1   The object of criminal work training is to ensure that the dog is capable of chasing and detaining an escaping criminal, defending the handler and/or itself against attack, disarming a criminal armed with a firearm or other weapon, guarding and escorting criminals after detention.

2   The importance of selecting a dog of good temperament is nowhere more fully illustrated than when training it for criminal work. The dog can be taught to be hard and firm towards a criminal and yet be perfectly natural and friendly with other people. Although undue friendliness with all and sundry must be frowned upon, this type of dog can, with correct training, become instantly hostile upon command and just as quickly revert to its basic good nature upon completion of its task. That is all that the needs of the police service demand. There is no justification in training a dog by unwise agitation to be in a state of permanent mistrust and suspicion. The aggressive or excessively sharp dog may well satisfy the early and misconceived ambitions of the novice handler. Unfortunately, very few, if any, have the ability to control this type of dog. Being in constant contact with the public, it will always be a source of worry and danger. On the other hand, timid and nervous animals can be built up to give the impression of fearlessness, particularly when they are on the lead or in close proximity to the handler, but it is entirely wrong to train such a dog.

3   The instructor engaged in the training of criminal work must fully appreciate the importance of the responsibilities involved. He must ensure that a sound foundation is established in the initial stages so that there is no danger of the dog becoming over aggressive or unreliable. Any assistant employed in this work must be fully experienced and dependable, otherwise any faultless act or omission could have permanent and undesirable consequences.

4   Handlers should always be aware of their individual responsibilities particularly when working a dog under operational conditions when it has been fully trained in criminal work. *An uncontrolled dog is as potentially dangerous as a loaded firearm.*

5   In criminal work training instructors and assistants require a certain amount of protective clothing. The amount used will depend on the age and temperament of the dog and the stage of training. In the initial training, the heavy protective suit or large padded arm should not be necessary. This will only encourage over aggression or, alternatively, the dog to reject the arm. A certain amount of protection is required but for

36

the training of young dogs it should be the minimum compatible with safety.

6 In training dogs for criminal work, care must be taken to avoid a build-up of an association with any sound, person, dress or terrain, and once the preliminary work has been accomplished there must be a constant change of 'criminals', training grounds and type of clothing worn. It is important for every action, both by handler and 'criminal', to be carried out in as practical a manner as possible. In this connection the questioning and releasing of suspects without any action being called for from the dog must be frequently carried out.

INITIAL STAGES CRIMINAL WORK TRAINING

Teasing with cloth

Initial bite on cloth

Tug o'war

Dog in possession

7 The beginning of the teaching of the 'chase' requires special attention as the utmost care must be taken to prevent undue excitement, hostility or apprehension on the part of the dog. Chasing must not under any circumstances be confined to the training ground alone. It must be carried out in such natural surroundings as roads, thoroughfares and gardens, and performed both by day and night. The part played by the 'criminal' is of the utmost importance and must be carried out in the initial stages by a highly experienced person. The 'criminal' should be dressed in ordinary clothes and any protection worn should be completely covered.

8   The dog is first quietly, on command, taught to hold and pull on a piece of strong cloth held by the instructor. The instructor should encourage the dog to pull him a few steps, then by momentarily resisting the pressure he will cause the dog to harden its grip. This is to be carried on until the dog is really gripping the cloth in a firm manner. At the same time the handler must give the dog plenty of encouragement. At this stage the command of *'leave'* is to be introduced and it is important that an immediate response to the command is obtained.

9   When the dog's grip is judged to be sufficiently firm, the same piece of cloth should be placed around the instructor's forearm with some of the cloth hanging loose. Again avoiding any excitement, the dog should be encouraged by the handler to grip and pull on the cloth as described above. As the training progresses the cloth is wrapped more firmly around the arm until only a small piece is hanging loose; this is to act as a stimulant to the dog.

10   Once the instructor is satisfied that the grip is clean and firm the next step of teaching the dog to tackle a running person is commenced. The dog, on the lead, is placed in the 'sit' position at the side of his handler. The instructor, with the cloth wrapped tightly around his arm, approaches and enters into conversation with the handler. After a short period he quietly turns and runs not too quickly from them. The handler waits for a brief moment to see that the dog does not anticipate a command. If no correction is needed he gives the *'stop him'* command. At the same time he runs with the dog and encourages it to grasp the arm of the instructor. At the beginning of this phase the arm may have to be fed to the dog but the necessity for this will soon end. Action may have to be taken by the instructor to get some dogs to bite firmly but the methods will vary with the individual dog. The distance the dog must run before it makes its attack should initially be short. The training must be carried out frequently, unless the dog is very receptive, and it should not be advanced until it can be relied upon to grip the 'criminal's' arm in a firm, clean and reliable manner. It is also important that the dog should leave the 'criminal's arm as soon as he gives up resistance or, if so trained, upon command. So far all this training will have been with the dog on the lead.

11   As soon as practicable the visual stimuli of the cloth should be abolished and an ordinary jacket with the minimum of protection introduced into the training. If care has been taken in the groundwork of the training of the chasing exercise, this stage will present few difficulties. If any do arise a prompt return to the appropriate stage in the introductory work is necessary.

12   Throughout the training of the 'chase and attack, exercise, dummy runs should be introduced. Under no circumstances must the dog be so trained that it anticipates a chase every time it sees a person running. It is essential for absolute control to be maintained from the start of the attack training and no slackening can be allowed if the result of this training is to be satisfactory.

Handler challenges suspect

Dog released

Dog in pursuit

Dog holding suspect

Handler searches suspect

Escort position

13 In all phases of the training the exercise must be completed by the interrogation, searching and escort of the 'criminal'.

14 In the final training with the dog in the 'sit' position, off the lead at the side of the handler, the 'criminal' will appear from some distance, dressed in normal clothing. He will be spoken to by the handler and after a short conversation the 'criminal' will turn and run. The handler will call upon him to stop. The 'criminal' will ignore him. The dog, which must have remained steady, is given the command *'stop him'*. The dog should unhesitatingly pursue him and should tackle him on the right arm in a clean and firm manner. The grip will be maintained until, according to the training, the 'criminal' stops running or when the dog is commanded to *'leave'* by the handler. The handler will place the 'criminal' between himself and the dog and search him. Finally he will call the dog to him and escort the 'criminal' away. The dog must have been trained in such a manner that as soon as the task of attack on the 'criminal' has been successfully completed it immediately ceases to be hostile.

Chase and stand-off

Word of Command: *'stop him'*

15 The object of this exercise is to ensure that on all occasions when a person surrenders by standing motionless, the dog will circle, bark and remain at a reasonable distance while at the same time keeping the person under surveillance until the arrival of the handler. This training should be carried out in conjunction with the 'search for person' exercise. It will give an added incentive to the dog and encourage barking, which is an essential part of the dog's training on locating a hidden person. It should not, however, be introduced until training in interrogation, search and escort, which must always be carried out when searching for hidden persons, has been mastered.

16 This exercise is a variation of the 'chase and attack' except that on this occasion the dog will not bite, but will contain the person pending interrogation by the handler.

17 The exercise will commence with the dog being in the 'heel free' position. The 'criminal' will attract the attention of the dog and run off at a moderate pace for a short distance at right angles from the dog rather than away from it. After a challenge to the 'criminal' from the handler, the dog will be released and simultaneously the 'criminal' will stand still. On arrival at the 'criminal' the dog should be encouraged to circle him and bark. The handler will then place the dog in the 'down' position and approach the 'criminal'. After a short conversation with him the handler will walk off with his dog in a direction different to that taken by the other man. On the first few occasions the dog may have a tendency to bite the 'criminal'. It will normally be possible to eliminate this fault with oral correction from the handler.

STAND OFF

Circling

Barking

Containing

18 Experience has shown that some form of restraint other than oral correction may be required to control the dog. The use of a long cord may be introduced if it fails to respond satisfactorily when the 'criminal' stands still. It must be appreciated that this must be used as a form of correction, not as a means of restricting the dog's movement or holding it away from

40

the 'criminal'. The cord should be jerked when correction is necessary and the tension immediately released. It may be of assistance that for the first few occasions after being freed of the cord, the check chain is left on the dog. In this way the association with the cord will be retained.

19 When the dog becomes more proficient at standing off and barking with the handler in close attendance, the distance can gradually be increased until the dog is capable of successfully completing this exercise in a variety of locations, circumstances and distances, including those in which both dog and 'criminal' are out of view.

Emergency stop

Word of Command: *'down'*

20 Nowhere in the sphere of police dog training is control more important than in all the man working exercises. It must, however, be realised that in operational police duty there will be circumstances where, having sent the dog to 'chase and attack' or 'chase and stand-off', it will be necessary to rescind these orders. Such circumstances should not arise very frequently but it is essential that the dog handler is able to call off his dog from such attacks.

21 Should action on these lines be necessary it must be realised that obedience is contrary to the nature of the dog.

22 No attempt should be made to include this training until the dog has reached a very high standard of proficiency in all the 'chase' exercises and it should not be practised to the detriment of those exercises.

23 The object of this exercise is to train the dog to cease chasing and adopt a 'down' position whilst keeping its quarry in view. It will already have been taught this positon during the obedience training (see Chapter 1). This exercise is an advancement on previous work in the 'criminal work' section and is included to increase the standard of control by the handler whilst working operationally.

24 In the initial stages, the handler with his dog 'heel free' will face the 'criminal' who will be standing 25 yards away, and following the procedure adopted for the 'stand-off' exercise, will run a short distance and on the release of the dog will immediately stand still. After the dog has run a few yards towards the 'criminal' the handler will give the command *'down'* when the dog should immediately respond by adopting the 'down' position. If for any reason the dog fails to react to the command, the handler, without any further commands, will go to it, put it on the lead, and take it to the original position where he will give it praise. This procedure will then be repeated until the dog is reacting instantly to the word of command. It will then be possible for the 'criminal' to continue running at a slow pace while the dog is held by command in the 'down' position. However, once again, if the dog fails to respond, the handler will, without further command, place his dog on the lead, take it back to the place of release and praise it.

25 When a satisfactory standard has been achieved at this stage of training, the distance between the handler and the 'criminal' can be gradually increased together with an increase of pace and the dog being allowed to pursue for a greater distance before being stopped by the command *'down'*.

26 It will now be possible for the 'criminal' to run in a direct line away from the handler and dog. If for any reason the dog does not respond to the command '*down*', the 'criminal' will immediately halt in order that the dog can be corrected accordingly. This will prevent any confusion by the dog receiving correction following its detention of a running 'criminal'.

27 Training in the exercise should always be carried out when the 'criminal' and dog are in view of the handler.

Chase in face of stick etc.
Word of Command *'stop him'*

CHASE IN FACE OF STICK ETC.

STICK

28 Training for this contingency will be similar to that used in the 'chase and attack' except that the 'criminal' will be armed with a stick and facing the dog.

Display of aggresssion by suspect

Dog sent

Dog attacks arm holding the weapon

Dog maintains firm grip

Handler in possession of weapon

29 The 'criminal' armed with a stick raised in a threatening manner will stand facing the handler and his dog. After a short pause, to ensure the dog only attacks on command, the dog will be ordered to attack. The 'criminal', still holding the stick, will run away to encourage the dog to bite on the right arm. Immediately the dog has a firm grip, the handler will command the 'criminal' to drop the weapon. The dog will, dependent upon its training, either leave the 'criminal's' arm when he desists or upon command. The normal interrogation, search and escort procedure should ensue.

30 Training should continue until the dog will attack *on command* in a determined manner under all conditions including when the 'criminal' is advancing in a threatening manner.

Chase in face of gun fire

31 The object of this exercise is to train the dog to attack and disarm a criminal armed with any type of firearm.

32 As soon as the dog is proficient in dealing with the 'criminal' armed with a stick, the training should be extended to deal with firearms. The *instructor* should be issued with a firearm for this purpose.

33 Should the dog display any apprehension in the 'chase and attack' when gunfire is introduced, the exercise should be carried out with an experienced and reliable dog within sight of the one under training. Action on these lines will normally result in the latter, having witnessed the chase and attack by another dog, quickly showing signs of a desire to participate. Once the initial reluctance has been overcome, practice as in the previous exercise should be continued until the dog attacks resolutely and without hesitation with the 'criminal' standing still or advancing towards the dog.

Escorting prisoners

34 It is essential after each 'chase and attack', 'chase and stand-off', and 'chasing in the face of stick and of gunfire', that the appropriate police action should be taken by the handler in order that the dog may associate its actions in the circumstances with the necessary 'follow-up' by the handler of interrogation, arrest and escort. In some practice exercises the 'follow-up' should include complete release of the person after interrogation.

35 When arrest and escort is practised, the distance over which the 'prisoner' is escorted should vary on each occasion, and should be made progressively longer. It is imperative that the dog is trained to watch the 'prisoner' closely. Should the dog show any lack of interest during escort it should be encouraged by a slight movement by the the 'prisoner' feigning escape. When the dog understands the purport of such action by the 'prisoner', a determined attempt to escape should be practised. The latter should, however, only be introduced into the practice occasionally.

36 The ideal position for the handler to assume when escorting a 'prisoner' is about 6 feet behind, with the dog at heel, off the lead. In this position both handler and dog have a clear view of the actions of the 'prisoner'. In addition, should the 'prisoner' attempt to escape, the dog is not likely to be impeded. Both handler and dog are thus out of range of any sudden kick or blow.

37 As an alternative, the dog can be trained to escort the 'criminal' by being positioned immediately behind him and slightly in front of the handler so that the escort can keep an eye on both the dog and the 'prisoner'.

38 The object of the training in this phase of its work is to ensure that the dog remains watchful so as to prevent any attempt at flight or violence.

Use of police dogs in crowd control situations
39 The Home Office Standing Advisory Committee on Police Dogs has considered the question of the extent of the use of police dogs in crowd control situations particularly in respect of football hooliganism. As a result, the following advice has been formulated:

i) The Committee has always recognised the use of police dogs in tracking after housebreakings, robberies, burglaries, searching premises to locate thieves, searching for missing persons, recovering articles at scenes of crime, assisting in combating rowdyism, chases after fleeing criminals, patrolling open spaces, general patrol, security and patrol duties.

ii) Dogs should not be used at political demonstrations or industrial meetings. They should never be used aggressively.

iii) Whereas it is accepted that dogs can deal effectively with small groups of hooligans, they should not normally be involved where there are large crowds assembled. Police dogs may well appear provocative and can become surrounded. In such circumstances, even if on a leash, they are liable to get excited and bite. This does not mean that they cannot be kept in reserve and out of sight, to be available in the event of serious disorder.

iv) There is no objection to police dogs being shown as deterrents at railway stations, car and coach parks, or along routes to football matches. However, their use in the ground at football matches is not advocated unless there are exceptional reasons.

Part II

Chapter 6

BREEDS OF DOGS

1 The use of dogs for police purposes has emphasised the need to produce an all-round dog in preference to a specialist dog. The varying circumstances under which police dogs have to be used have confirmed that to be successful, a police dog must have intelligence of a high order, boldness and keenness of the senses. Its build should be sturdy with the physical ability to perform hard work under all climatic conditions.

2 Within the general qualifications mentioned, the following breeds have been trained successfully for police work in this country and on the continent:

Alsatian (German Shepherd Dog)
Airedale
Boxer
Rottweiller
Dobermann
Labrador
Bouvier
Reisenschnauzer
Wiemaraner

3 The most suitable all-purpose dog so far used for police purposes is the Alsatian or German Shepherd Dog. This breed possesses all the physical attributes considered essential and, in addition, its reputation (albeit unfounded) has a salutary psychological effect on would-be wrongdoers.

4 It is comparatively difficult to obtain sufficient numbers of Alsatian dogs of the high standard required to meet the evergrowing demands of the police service. It is, therefore, necessary to explore the potentialities of other suitable breeds.

5 The staffs of existing training establishments for police dogs are constantly engaged in experimenting with various breeds which fulfil the basic requirements, and the results of experiments may well at some future date result in the introduction of more breeds for training. The experimental work referred to is frequently prolonged and it is in the best interests of the police service as a whole, that such experiments should be confined to established training centres.

Chapter 7

ACQUISITION OF DOGS

1 The detail of necessary training to produce a dog suitable in all respects for police work shown in Part 1, Chapters 1 to 5, indicates the paramount importance of the knowledge and care required in the initial selection of animals for the training course. There can be no hard and fast rule as affecting any particular breed as individual dogs of any breed vary considerably in their mental approach to the training, and in their ability to assimilate such training. It is, therefore, stressed that the selection of dogs considered suitable for training as police dogs must be based on experience and must be done with extreme care. It must be appreciated that shortcomings in any individual dog may not become apparent until the training is well advanced. No useful purpose will ever be served by persevering with dogs which are in any way lacking the essential qualifications.

2 The present and future requirements of the police service may be met in two ways, viz:
  i by breeding at authorised breeding establishments; and
  ii by acquiring young dogs at an age suitable to commence or be prepared for training.

3 Chapters 8 and 9 deal at some length with the problem of breeding and indicate that the results of breeding must still be carefully scrutinised before selection for training.

4 There is some divergence of opinion as to the best age at which training should begin, but experience has shown that the best results are obtained if training is undertaken when the dogs are between 12 and 18 months old. Thus, in considering the question of breeding for police purposes, the long unproductive up-bringing of puppies must be taken into account.

5 An alternative to direct breeding for police purposes is the acquisition of suitable dogs at or near the age when they are ready to begin training.

Chapter 8

BREEDING, MATING AND CARE OF PUPPIES AFTER WEANING

Breeding

1 Although the police service is not concerned with producing dogs for show purposes, a dog that looks its breed must obviously be the ultimate aim of police dog breeding. In endeavouring to secure this aim, care must be taken that nothing is introduced to the detriment of the character that is required.

2 In considering breeding, a careful study should be made of the pedigree of the dog and bitch it is proposed to mate. Where possible an ancestor whose type and characteristics it is desired to reproduce, should be common at least once, but preferably more often in each pedigree. It can be expected normally that the dog and bitch will each contribute 50 per cent towards the offspring, but the ancestor which is common to both will usually be a dominant factor.

3 This method of approach is known as Line Breeding. The more lines that run to a particular dog, the more likely it is that this type of dog will be reproduced. Care is, however, necessary, to avoid the danger of incest breeding, which, although sometimes highly successful, can be equally disastrous.

4 Dark colours are preferred for police dogs; pale colours should not, therefore, be mated together. A light coloured dog or bitch should, if possible, be mated to an opposite, not only of darker, richer colouring but also bred from parents of such colouring.

5 Faults such as long coats, overshot jaws, missing teeth, soft ears, light eyes can normally be bred out by careful selection of parents known by their blood lines to be free of such faults.

Stud dog

6 The stud dog should closely approach the standard of the breed and must possess all the qualities required in a police dog, and if possible, come from a long line of suitable working dogs.

7 A study of the influence his ancestors may be expected to have on his progeny must be made in order to assess his immediate suitability to the bitch. In mating for temperament care should be taken that the combined temperaments are suitable. Shy or jumpy dogs should not be used for breeding purposes.

8 The stud dog should enjoy robust health and should normally be about two years old for his first bitch which should, if possible, be an experienced matron. A good stud dog may be expected to serve bitches until he is at least six years old.

Brood bitch

9 The qualities of the stud dog apply equally to the brood bitch; in addition, the bitch should possess a deep roomy body. Narrow-hipped bitches are considered unsuitable for breeding however good their pedigree and working qualities.

10 The bitch's third season can be expected when she is between 18 months and 2 years old. This is the best time for her first mating. She should not be mated every season; it is reasonable to expect that the bitch will raise a healthy litter of puppies if she is mated every other season. She should not be expected to raise more than 6 litters during her life.

Mating

11 Under normal conditions, a bitch can be expected to come in season about every 6 months; this may, however, vary. Some bitches may miss a season altogether, whilst others may produce a season every 3 or 4 months. The season can be expected to last for 3 weeks. The first appearance is the swelling of the vulva with a colourless discharge which gradually darkens to the colour of blood. The swelling gradually becomes more and more pronounced. The discharge and swelling will continue for about a week; the vulva will gradually soften and become slightly open. It is at this stage, which is usually about the tenth day of the season, that the bitch is ready for mating.

12 It is unlikely that she will stand for a dog before this stage is reached but there are exceptions; on rare occasions a bitch may accept a dog before the tenth day.

13 A reliable sign that a bitch is ready for mating is when she shows signs of sexual excitement when she is stroked on the back just forward of the tail; she will often hold her tail to one side and raise the vulva.

14 The best time for mating is considered to be between the twelfth and sixteenth day, and although it should not be necessary, it is advisable that two matings should be made.

15 Some trouble in the actual mating of the bitch may be expected if she is a maiden, and particularly if she is quite mature. A bitch in the police service whose training has denied her the usual freedom with other dogs may be particularly difficult.

16 The dog and bitch should be introduced and allowed to get to know each other; it may only be a few minutes before they are mated, but if necessary the bitch can be on a lead and the dog free. The ground surface should not be slippery.

17 If the dog is heavy and the bitch cannot support him, it will be necessary to help by supporting her underneath. When mating has taken place, wait a few moments and keep the bitch as still as possible. When they are 'tied' lift the front legs of the dog from the bitch and place them so that they are back to back. It is advisable to remain with them whilst they are 'tied' so as to be in a position to hold them still if the bitch tries to struggle. The 'tie' will usually last between 10 and 20 minutes. When they separate they should be kennelled and allowed to rest.

18 The recognised procedure for matings is that the bitch is taken to the dog; if the mating is unsuccessful a free mating, at the next season, is usually given.

Care of bitches in whelp

19 It will normally be about 4 or 5 weeks after the mating before it is possible to tell if the bitch is in whelp. The first indication that she is will be her appetite; she will be very inconsistent with her food, inclined to vomit and will have less control over her bowels. About the fifth week there will be an obvious increase in the size of the flanks and she will start to fill with milk. The presence of the milk will be less obvious in a maiden bitch.

20 Up to the sixth week no difference in the usual activities or diet is necessary. From the start of the sixth week, however, her diet should include about $2\frac{1}{2}$ pounds of meat daily in 2 or 3 feeds, plus milk and eggs. She should have plenty of exercise but jumping and similar violent exercises likely to do harm should be avoided.

21 The bitch should be kennelled where she is expected to whelp at least a week before whelping takes place. The kennel should have a wooden floor and be situated in a run. It must be draught proof and kept at an even temperature. The kennel should be kept scrupulously clean at all times. Although the bitch can be expected to start whelping 63 days after mating, they are often early.

22 Sacking, which should be fastened down to the flooring, is the most suitable bedding on which to whelp.

23 There will be about half an hour between the birth of each puppy. After each birth the bitch will be busy cleaning up and clearing the puppy from the bag (or caul) in which it is born. For this reason, straw or similar bedding should be avoided. In some cases, if the bitch is weak, it may be necessary to break the caul to prevent the puppy from being drowned or suffocated.

24 Veterinary assistance should be sought immediately if there are any complications.

25 In a normal whelping the bitch is best left alone. The handler or kennelman familiar to her may be present but strangers should be kept away.

26 The bitch will probably not leave her puppies for the first two days except to relieve herself, but she should be in a position to do so if she wishes.

27 If the litter numbers more than 6, it should be reduced to that number. Examination of the puppies on the day following whelping will reveal the weakest and those of unwanted sex.

28 It is likely that the puppies will be born without dewclaws on their hind legs; if present they should be removed about the third day. It is also advisable to have dewclaws on the forelegs removed.

29 For the first 24 hours after whelping the bitch should be fed on a light diet of milk and raw eggs. After this, the diet as before whelping may be resumed. While she is lactating she will need to be very well fed. She should be in a position to be able to get away from the puppies for periods and not be confined with them all the time. About once a week the puppies' toenails should be cut as they become very sharp and cause the bitch considerable discomfort; the puppies eyes should open after approximately 10 days.

30 At the end of the third week the puppies will start to grow milk teeth and the process of weaning, which should be extended over about 3 weeks, may begin. The bitch should be removed from the puppies for certain hours during the day. Her absences should be gradually extended until she is with them only long enough to give them a feed in the morning and evening.

31 Throughout the weaning period the puppies should be introduced to a light diet of raw meat. Initially about one tablespoonful of raw, scraped or finely minced meat 3 times daily should suffice. The amount should be gradually increased until, by the time they are independent of the bitch, their diet is about 1 pound a day in 4 feeds. At the same time that meat is introduced, the puppies may be given a feed of milk and cereal.

32 As the bitch is gradually removed from the puppies they will lack her warmth, particularly at night. The bitch will be completely removed by the eighth week. To compensate for this the bedding should be altered accordingly. Bedding consisting of clean straw changed regularly is recommended.

33 Throughout the whelping and the period during which the bitch is feeding the puppies, careful watch should be kept on the general health of the brood bitch. In particular, daily examination of the teats is necessary for traces of any swelling or abscesses. Veterinary assistance should be secured without delay as necessary.

Care of puppies after weaning

34 When puppies are sent out from the Breeding Establishments, they should, wherever possible, be boarded with established or potential handlers. It is important that the litter should be split up between the eighth and in any case not longer than the tenth week. Puppies running together after this age develop the 'pack' habit and when ultimately separated they may develop unsatisfactory habits.

35 The upbringing of puppies is of paramount importance to ensure that the physical and mental development is guided to meet the requirements of the animals' service life. Physically, the main object is to build up a sound bone structure, whilst mentally, care is necessary to avoid characteristics or habits which will be adverse to subsequent training for police purposes.

36 Apart from the necessary features of diet calculated to assist physical development and a watchful care on the general health, puppies require little assistance in the growing-up process. In a litter as a whole or individually, they will normally get all the exercise they need initially by their own resources in the correct surroundings. Care should be taken to allow adequate rest and in no circumstances should they be over-exercised. In a natural state puppies will exercise themselves by play to the limit of their endurance; nature will dictate the need for sleep.

37 No attempt should be made to anticipate the eventual training course other than to associate the young dogs with human beings. It will be found that they will quickly associate themselves with the person responsible for their feeding and general well-being; at this stage a natural confidence in humans will be established without any set method of instruction.

38 As the dogs mature towards the age at which they are ready for training, steps should be taken to introduce them to the wearing of collars, etc. Sensible controlled romping and play with a piece of stout cloth to encourage a mouth hold may be indulged in with the limited object of developing confidence.

39 Cases in which puppies are boarded out require careful consideration. Every account of the home conditions of the potential handler should be taken to avoid circumstances where the free development of the puppy may be impaired. Although no police training is to be undertaken at this stage, it is important that no influences or habits are encountered which will be detrimental to subsequent training.

40 The Sub-Committee formed for the study of all aspects of dog breeding meets frequently at one or other of the Dog Breeding Establishments. It is hoped that it will be freely consulted on any matter connected with the breeding programme.

Chapter 9

SELECTION OF DOGS

Breed requirements of an Alsatian

Characteristics

1 The characteristic expression of the Alsatian gives the impression of perpetual vigilance, fidelity, liveliness and watchfulness, alert to every sight and sound, with nothing escaping attention; fearless, but with decided suspiciousness of strangers – as opposed to the immediate friendliness of some breeds. The Alsatian possesses highly developed senses, mentally and temperamentally. He should be strongly individualistic and possess a high standard of intelligence. Three of the most outstanding traits are incorruptibility, discernment and ability to reason.

General appearance

2 The general appearance of the Alsatian is a well-proportioned dog showing great suppleness of limb, neither massive nor heavy, but at the same time free from any suggestion of weediness. It must not approach the greyhound type. The body is rather long, strongly boned, with plenty of muscle, obviously capable of endurance and speed and of quick and sudden movement. The gait should be supple, smooth and long-reaching, carrying the body along with the minimum of up-and-down movement, entirely free from stiltedness.

Head and skull

3 The head is proportionate to the size of the body, long, lean and clean-cut, broad at the base of the skull, but without coarseness, tapering to the nose with only a slight stop between the eyes. The skull is slightly domed and the top of the nose should be parallel to the forehead. The cheek must not be full or in any way prominent and the whole head when viewed from the top should be much in the form of a V, well filled in under the eyes. There should be plenty of substance in foreface, with a good depth from top to bottom. The muzzle is strong and long and, while tapering to the nose, it must not be carried to such an extreme as to give the appearance of being overshot. It must not show any weakness, or be snipy or lippy. The lips must be tight fitting and clean. The nose must be black.

Eyes

4 The eyes are almond-shaped, as nearly as possible matching the surrounding coat but darker rather than lighter in shade and placed to look straight forward. They must not be in any way bulging or prominent, and must show a lively, alert and highly intelligent expression.

Ears
5 The ears should be of moderate size, but rather large than small, broad at the base and pointed at the tips, placed rather high on the skull and carried erect – all adding to the alert expression of the dog as a whole. (It should be noted, in case novice breeders may be misled, that in Alsatian puppies the ears often hang until the age of 6 months and sometimes longer, becoming erect with the replacement of the milk teeth.)

Mouth
6 The teeth should be sound and strong, gripping with a scissor-like action, the lower incisors just behind, but touching the upper.

Neck
7 The neck should be strong, fairly long with plenty of muscle, fitting gracefully into the body, joining the head without sharp angles and free from throatiness.

Forequarters
8 The shoulders should slope well back. The ideal being that a line drawn through the centre of the shoulder blade should form a right angle with the humerus when the leg is perpendicular to the ground in stance. Upright shoulders are a major fault. They should show plenty of muscle, which is distinct from, and must not be confused with coarse or loaded bone, which is a fault. The shoulder-bone should be clean. The forelegs should be perfectly straight viewed from the front, but the pasterns should show a slight angle with the forearm when regarded from the side; too great an angle denotes weakness and, while carrying plenty of bone, it should be of good quality. Anything approaching the massive bone of the Newfoundland, for example, is a decided fault.

Body
9 The body is muscular, the back is broadish and straight, strongly boned and well developed. The body shows a waist without being tucked up. There should be a good depth of brisket or chest, the latter should not be too broad. The sides are flat compared with some breeds, and while the dog must not be barrel-ribbed, it must not be so flat as to be actually slabsided. The Alsatian should be quick in movement and speedy but not like a Greyhound in body.

Hindquarters
10 The hindquarters should show breadth and strength, the loins being broad and strong, the rump rather long and sloping and the legs, when viewed from behind, must be quite straight, without any tendency to cow-hocks or bow-hocks, which are both extremely serious faults. The stifles are well turned and the hocks strong and well let down. The ability to turn quickly is a necessary asset to the Alsatian, and this can only be if there is a good length of thigh-bone and leg, and by the bending of the hock.

Feet

11 The feet should be round, the toes strong, slightly arched and held close together. The pads should be firm, the nails short and strong. Dewclaws are neither a fault nor a virtue, but should be removed from the hind legs at 4 to 5 days old, as they are liable to spoil the gait.

Tail

12 When at rest the tail should hang in a slight curve, and reach at least as far as the hock. During movement and excitement it will be raised, but in no circumstances should the tail be carried past a vertical line drawn through the root.

Coat

13 The coat is smooth, but it is at the same time a double coat. The undercoat is woolly in texture, thick and close, and to it the animal owes its characteristic resistance to cold. The outer coat is also close, each hair straight, hard and lying flat, so that it is rain resisting. Under the body, to behind the legs, the coat is longer and forms near the thigh a mild form of breaching. On the head (including the inside of the ears), to the front of the legs and feet, the hair is short. Along the neck it is longer and thicker. A coat either too long or too short is a fault. As an average, the hairs on the back should be from 1 to 2 inches in length.

Colour

14 The colour of the Alsatian is in itself not important and has no effect on the character of the dog or on its fitness for work and should be a secondary consideration for that reason. All white or near white, unless possessing black points, are not desirable. The final colour of a young dog can only be ascertained when the outer coat has developed.

Size

15 The ideal height (measured to the highest point of the shoulder) is 22–24 inches for bitches and 24–26 inches for dogs. The proportion of length to height may vary between 10:9 and 10:8·5.

Faults

16 A long narrow Collie or Borzoi head. A pink or liver-coloured nose. Undershot or overshot mouth. Tail with a pronounced hook. The lack of heavy undercoat.

Breed requirements of a Dobermann

Head

17 The head is rather long and very clean in line, only a very moderate width in skull, and generally slender in design, running through a slight stop to a wedge-shaped muzzle.

Eyes

18 The eyes are medium in size and are round and dark brown, with a lively and inquisitive expression.

Ears

19 The ears are set rather high, are moderate in size, and carried erect and slightly forward. The German specimens (and many others in other countries, including some States of the USA) are, of course, cropped to a point.

Muzzle

20 The muzzle is wedge-shaped and has jaws that are rather lean without being at all snipy, clean in lip and outline, well muscled and possessed of good level teeth.

Neck

21 The neck is obviously powerful and carries the head high in the air, yet with its very slight arch is a graceful organ which, joining to a body of such lissom and symmetrical lines, enhances the handsomeness of the whole.

Back

22 The back is rather short, quite straight and firm and of moderate width.

Body properties

23 The chest is deep and adequately roomy without being barrelled. The loins are sufficiently lifted and the couplings powerfully linked. The legs are all good length, straight, rather well boned and muscled, and having rather small compact feet (the forefeet are almost cat like).

Tail

24 The tail is set in line with the back, moderately thick at the root, and docked to quite a short stump.

Coat

25 The coat is smooth and rather short on the head and legs, though a trifle harsh in texture on the body generally, flat and close lying. In colour, it is black with slight tan pencillings and eye spots, or black, tan, or blue with red points. (White is not permitted except as a small blur on the chest or brisket.)

Height and weight

26 The height is generally about 25 inches, and the weight approximately 45 pounds.

General appearance

27 In general, the Dobermann is a fine upstanding dog of fearless character and unusual intelligence and one which is in appearance like an improved edition of the Old Manchester Terrier.

Physical structure of the dog

28 A dog cannot adequately perform the tasks required of him unless he has the correct structure and physical attributes to make it possible. It is essential, therefore, that police dog handlers should have a basic knowledge of the standards of a good working police dog. Apart from general good health, which is a primary consideration, here are some points to look for:

i NOSE   The point of the nose should be dark, or at least blend with the general colouring. Any outstanding paleness indicates a weakness.

ii MOUTH   The lower incisors should fall just behind, but touching, the incisors of the upper jaw and all the teeth should, of course, be sound and free from discolouration. Common faults are 'undershot' jaws in which the lower incisors extend beyond the upper, and 'overshot' when the upper incisors are too far in front of the lower ones.

iii EYES   The colour of the eye should blend nicely with the colour of the surrounding coat. It should be bright and clear without any sign of discharge, whether watery or otherwise. A common fault is a light or glaring eye.

iv EARS   Some breeds have an erect ear carriage, whilst in others the ears naturally droop or hang. In breeds with an erect ear carriage, such as the Alsatian, the adult dog's ears should be erect and carried high on the skull. Any form of drooping is a bad fault, as correct ear carriage has a lot to do with a dog's alert expression and his ability to convey useful information to his handler.
The following diagram illustrates good and bad types:

FOREQUARTERS

Correct   Bad   Bad

v FOREQUARTERS   The shoulder blades should form a right angle with the humerus when the dog is standing squarely, if it is to have an easy action and correct gait. Any variation, such as a straight shoulder, is a bad fault in a working dog because it inhibits free action and thus causes early fatigue.

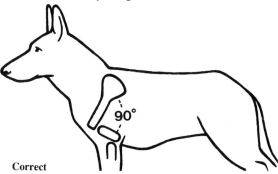

Correct

57

The forelegs should be straight when viewed from the front, any variation from which will make the dog walk improperly.

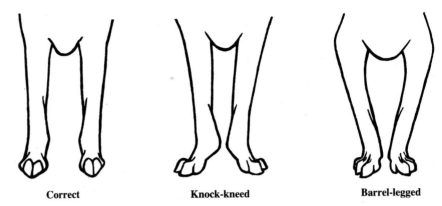

Correct   Knock-kneed   Barrel-legged

The chest should be both wide and deep to give plenty of room to the respiratory organs.

   vi   FEET The toes should be strong, slightly arched, and close together. Dewclaws are not regarded as a fault on the feet, but should be removed from the back feet. The commonest fault is known as 'hare' foot, which is illustrated below:

FEET

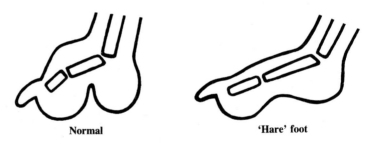

Normal   'Hare' foot

   vii BACK The back should be strong and straight. Weakness is shown in the form of a hollow back as illustrated hereunder.

BACK

viii HINDQUARTERS The hindquarters should give the impression of strength and power, and the hind legs should be straight. Some of the commoner defects are shown in the following diagram:

Cow-hocked **Barrel-legged** **Knock-kneed**

ix TAIL In the case of the Alsatian, the tail should hang downwards in a slight curve, although if the dog is moving or excited it may be carried higher. Definite faults in tail carriage are illustrated below:

Bad **Bad**

x COAT The desirable coat is short haired on top with a close woolly textured undercoat. A really good undercoat is an important feature in the Alsatian.

Chapter 10

KENNELLING

1   Kennels may be of a permanent or temporary character but in both cases must conform to basic standards. Those provided at Training Establishments or other centres where numbers of dogs are to be kept should preferably be permanent structures. Kennels provided for use at the homes of handlers should be of temporary character to enable dismantling and removal as necessary.

2   Basically all types of kennelling should be:

   i   water-tight and wind proof;

   ii   adequately ventilated. Draughts should be avoided;

   iii   of appropriate size to permit the dog to stand up or lie down in comfort.

Permanent kennels

3   Considerable care must be taken in the correct siting of kennels. Quietness and good drainage are essential. Due consideration must be given to the proximity of the training areas.

4   Each kennel should communicate with an outside run and should be equipped with a removable bed-board raised a few inches off the ground. The fall of the floor should be such that all water runs into gutters which connect with outside traps. No stagnant water or sewage should be allowed to collect inside the kennels. Experience has shown that the use of concrete is not advisable.

5   All kennel blocks should be provided with the maximum of natural light for the benefit of the health of the dogs. An electric light system should be installed additionally.

6   No artificial heating for general kennels is necessary. Provided the kennel has been properly constructed, the natural thickening of the coat in winter, plus the addition of bedding should be sufficient to maintain the body heat of the healthy dog. Thin-coated dogs may be provided with a dog coat. (See also Isolation and Hospital Kennels.)

7   Provision should be made in all multiple kennel sites for suitable cooking and storage facilities. A refrigerator to store meat is a great asset (see also para. 18). Ideally, a veterinary room, equipped with bench, cupboards and ablution facilities should be provided.

8   In training school compounds, necessary administration, classroom, store-room, canteen facilities, drying, changing and toilet rooms, and garage accommodation should be included.

Temporary kennels

9 Whilst conforming to the basic requirements, it is recommended that temporary kennels should be of wooden sectional construction. The same care as to siting, etc., is necessary as for permanent kennels. Where possible, temporary kennels should be sited on hard standings, but if this is impracticable, well drained ground should be chosen. To obviate the possibility of dampness seeping through the floor, the kennel should have legs which raise it at least 6 inches from the ground. Temporary kennels should be placed in such a position that the closed ends face the prevailing wind.

Bedding

10 The provision of bedding is limited to giving additional warmth in cold weather and to prevent bed-sores in thin coated dogs. Straw (avoiding badly broken straw) and wood shavings are suitable bedding material which should be shaken up daily and removed and burnt as necessary.

Hospital and isolation kennels

11 To ensure the proper care and treatment of sick dogs a hospital block incorporating a veterinary surgeon's room should be provided on the basis of 5 per cent of the total number of dogs at the establishment. Separate cooking facilities are recommended.

12 Isolation kennels for the sole use of dogs suffering or suspected to be suffering from infectious or contagious disease should be provided at some distance from the main kennels. New entrants should be treated as suspects. Administrative conditions should be such as to avoid contact between personnel necessarily using the isolation block and other personnel on the establishment.

13 Whenever it is proposed to kennel dogs subject to quarantine regulations, arrangements as approved by the Ministry of Agriculture, Fisheries and Food must be adopted.

Chapter 11

KENNEL MANAGEMENT

General

1 Kennels should be thoroughly cleaned daily. All soiled bedding and excreta should be removed and burnt. Bed-boards should be scrubbed weekly, care being taken to ensure that they are completely dry before return to the kennels. Because excessive dampness may induce symptoms of rheumatism to which dogs are prone, the indiscriminate washing down of kennels should be avoided. In wet weather and in winter especially, the free use of water should be reduced to a minimum consistent with cleanliness.

2 Dogs are very susceptible to carbolic poisoning and for this reason the use of the carbolic group of disinfectants should normally be very limited; in all cases any such preparation should be carefully diluted. Where, owing to the presence of an infectious or contagious disease, thorough disinfecting is necessary, it will be found that intense heat is the most reliable form; where its use does not incur the risk of fire, it should be employed by means of a blow-lamp. In wooden kennels, however, a reliable disinfectant preparation will be used.

3 All brick walls, floors and iron work should be thoroughly flamed with a blow-lamp. Bed-boards, feeding utensils, grooming brushes etc., should be thoroughly washed and left out in the sun to dry.

4 Even after a kennel has been disinfected, it is advisable in the interests of hygiene to leave it empty if possible for 14 days.

Grooming

5 A dog should be thoroughly groomed each day. Apart from cleaning the coat and skin, regular grooming helps to keep both in a healthy condition. Grooming provides one of the most useful opportunities for the handler to become thoroughly acquainted with his dog; it also enables examination to be made for wounds and skin troubles. Opportunity should be taken for regular inspection of the eyes, teeth, ears, nails and anus.

6 The Alsatian dog, like some other breeds, has two coats – a soft woolly undercoat close to the skin and an outer coat consisting of longer, coarser hair. Cleaning of the coat and skin should be done with a brush and comb. The dog should at first be given a vigorous massage with the tips of the fingers to stimulate circulation in the skin. The coat should then be brushed at first against and then with the direction of the growth of the hair. The comb should be used to remove dead and tangled hair; care should be taken to ensure the comb does not bring away too much top or undercoat.

This is especially important during the winter when the dog is dependent on both its coats for body warmth.

Bathing

7 Provided the daily grooming is properly carried out it should seldom be necessary to bath a dog. Frequent bathing is likely to remove the natural grease in the skin and coat to the detriment of the health and appearance of the dog.

8 If, in the interests of cleanliness bathing is necessary, water not exceeding 100 degrees F. should be used. Steps should be taken to prevent soap entering the eyes and ears. All traces of soap should be removed from the coat by thorough rinsing. Care must also be taken to thoroughly dry the dog with towels or chamois leathers. In warm weather, the dog may be encouraged to run about outside but on no account should it be exposed to inclement weather until it is properly dried.

Feeding

9 Adult dogs should be fed once a day and, to avoid any disturbance of the digestive processes, they should be fed at the same time daily. If possible, the feed should not be given immediately before or after work and, in hot weather, it is advisable to avoid feeding during the heat of the day.

10 In training establishments the feed should be given late in the afternoon in order to allow sufficient time after feeding for the dogs to empty themselves before being kennelled for the night. Action on these lines will develop regular habits and will lessen kennel fouling.

11 Water is essential to the health of the dog at all times. A plentiful supply of fresh clean water should be always available. Dogs should be taken to the water and the vessels emptied after drinking and only refilled when next taken to the water.

Diet

12 The food of all dogs must be balanced to ensure:
   i)   that it is palatable;
   ii) that it supplies the energy need of the dog;
   iii) that it contains the necessary protein, vitamins and mineral.

13 Meat and other high protein foods such as fish should constitute approximately one-half of the total ration. It may be fed raw or cooked. Most dogs prefer raw meat but it will be found that cooked meat is more easily mixed with the other components of the ration. When fish is fed as a substitute for meat, great care must be taken to ensure that all bones are removed before it is given to the dog.

14 Bones are not an essential part of the diet. If they are included, only large beef bones should be provided; on no account should bones that splinter such as lamb or poultry bones be given.

15 Biscuits provide the essential carbo-hydrate constituent of the ration in addition to being an aid to digestion and should constitute approximately one-third of it. Oats and dried bread (toasted) may be substituted for biscuits.

16 Vegetables provide essential minerals and vitamins and should constitute approximately one-sixth of the ration. All varieties of green vegetables are suitable but some difficulty may be experienced in getting the dog to eat them. Root crops such as parsnips and carrots are very suitable and should be minced or chopped small, uncooked, for mixing with the rest of the feed.

17   An average working Alsation dog should have a daily ration of:

Meat	24 oz
Biscuits	16 oz
Vegetables	8 oz

Preparation of food

18   All food should be prepared as near the feeding time as possible and, when served, the dogs should be left alone to consume it. Food bowls should be removed from the kennels after about 15 minutes and all unconsumed food disposed of. Only in the case of known shy feeders should food be left in the kennel. Meat kept in refrigerators must be completely thawed before being fed to the dogs.

19   All feedings utensils should be thoroughly washed after use.

Exercise

20   Within the limitations of training and/or working commitments, it is necessary that every dog should receive regular daily exercise to maintain its healthy condition. The exercise may be either free or organised but no adult dog who is not under the complete control of the handler should be given free exercise in the presence of other dogs. In appropriate cases some free exercise should be allowed before kennelling for the night, and as early as possible in the morning.

Dogs kennelled at the home of the handler

21   All the above instructions should be carried out by a handler with a police dog kennelled at his home; particular attention should be paid to the feed times in relation to the work performed. Much of the necessary exercise will be performed as part of the patrol duty.

Chapter 12

EQUIPMENT

Equipment may be conveniently divided into 3 categories:
 i)   kennel equipment
 ii) training equipment
 iii) general

(i) Kennel equipment

Each kennel should be provided with:

a) feeding bowl consisting of a rustless metal bowl sufficiently large (8 inches in diameter and $2\frac{1}{2}$ inches deep) to hold the feed and broad enough at the base (10 inches in diameter) to prevent it being tipped up in use;

b) water bowl of similar type as the feeding bowl;

c) hard stiff grooming brush;

d) a softer finishing brush;

e) a metal comb;

f) a clinical thermometer (individual issue for dogs at homes of handlers);

g) a dumb-bell;

h) a muzzle;

i) chamois leather;

j) brushes;

k) shovels;

l) incinerator;

(ii) Training equipment

Each handler should be equipped with:

a) choke chain. This should be rustless, linked chain. One swivel link should be incorporated. Large links are recommended to avoid any tendency of the links to cut into the skin or cut the hair on the neck of the dog. All links and loops should be welded.

b) leather collar;

c) leather lead. This should be of strong leather approximately 4 feet long and $\frac{7}{8}$ inch wide with hand loop and collar attachment. The lead should be capable of adjustment to length by spring-loaded clips;

d) tracking harness. May be of leather or webbing, and should be capable of adjustment to size of neck and girth of dog;

e) tracking line. Should be plaited line at least 30 feet long, bonded at each end, and equipped with fastener for attachment to tracking harness.

(iii) General

Hurdles
Normal athletic type hurdles capable of adjustment in height are recommended for initial jumping instruction. Additional provision of natural obstacles such as low brick walls, privet hedges, etc., will be necessary for later training stages.

Scramble-Board
Of wooden construction, two faces being hinged together so that the angle at the apex can be adjusted. The face boards should be tongued and grooved with 'V' shaped edges and fixed horizontally to provide some grip for the dog.

The overall height can be lowered thus increasing the apex angle for the training of young dogs.

For competition use, the overall height should be 6 feet and, with the overall distance between the two legs at the base at $42\frac{1}{2}$ inches the angle at the apex will be approximately 30°.

Firearms
Various calibre from .22 to .45 Blank ammunition.

Protective clothing
As necessary.

Chapter 13

DOG HANDLERS

1 The careful selection of men suitable for training as dog handlers is vital to the successful employment of dogs for police purposes. At all stages of training and operational use, the handler and the dog work as a team, often with the minimum of supervision. The selection of suitable personnel for training is, therefore, no less important than the careful selection of dogs.

2 Men to be considered for training as dog handlers must be sound, experienced policemen whose mental alertness, equable temperament and willingness to persevere are above average. The nature of the training and subsequent operational work calls for a high standard of physical fitness.

3 Previous experience with animals may well be an advantage but the lack of it is not necessarily a disqualification in the case of an otherwise suitable officer. It is important, however, that a handler should have a forceful character with a determination to succeed and a cheerful disposition which will be reflected subsequently in the behaviour of his dog. A handler of a brusque or nagging disposition will confuse and may easily ruin a dog.

4 In cases where a police dog is to be kennelled at the home of the handler, serious consideration should be given to the home background and, in particular, to home ties. It is essential to ensure that no disruption of the family life of the handler will result, and that the general atmosphere of the household is placid. Adequate kennelling facilities must be available in a position where interference with and disturbance of the dog is minimised.

5 The devotion of the handler to the dog and to duty must be without question; the former will ensure a mutual confidence and respect which will be shown in the dog's attitude to work, and the latter is an operational necessity more especially in areas where the number of police dogs is small.

6 The technical ability of a handler can only be really judged after he has been allocated a dog for a 'Familiarisation Course', or when he commences full training.

Chapter 14

INSTRUCTORS

1 Instructors for police dogs and handlers must necessarily be considered in two classes, viz:

    i)   for training establishments; and

    ii) for refresher training.

2 The basic qualifications for each class should be identical to ensure continuity of training and techniques.

3 The initial training and subsequent refresher training of both dogs and handlers is specialised work which calls for a high standard of instruction at all stages. Instructors should therefore:

    i)   be of sound judgement with above average qualities of leadership;

    ii) possess a sound knowledge of all aspects of dog training for police purposes;

    iii) be experienced in the operational use of police dogs.

4 Instructors employed at training establishments should also have the ability to import knowledge and to demonstrate and should possess additionally sound experience in:

    i)   the care of dogs;

    ii) kennel management;

    iii) judging dogs for temperament and conformity;

    iv) breeding

5 Officers employed as Instructors for refresher training should have facilities for maintaining close liaison with the Instructor at the training establishment responsible for the initial training of all dogs under his supervision.

6 Instructors' Courses are organised under the auspices of the Standing Advisory Committee on Police Dogs. Successful candidates are awarded certificates as Accredited Instructors.

Chapter 15

CLASSROOM WORK

1 The necessary training to produce a trained police dog and handler consists of:
  i) the practical work done by the handler and dog together;
  ii) the theoretical instruction given to the handler.

The former is normally performed in various parts of the training ground area; the latter constitutes classroom work. Much of the practical work must receive individual instruction and supervision; theoretical instruction may be given in classes.

2 Lectures by qualified instructors should include:
  i) Introduction to training and general principles involved;
  ii) Care of dog; examination and grooming;
  iii) Feeding and hygiene;
  iv) Equipment, care and use;
  v) Basic anatomy of dogs;
  vi) Theory of scent; tracking, searching, etc;
  vii) Operational use of police dogs;
  viii) Refresher training; maintenance of standards.

Opportunity should be given in all lecture periods for questions and discussion.

3 Each curriculum should include at least one lecture by a qualified Veterinary Surgeon.

Aids to instruction

4 The provision of aids to instruction, e.g., films, slides, diagrams, charts, etc., is recommended.

Classroom equipment

5 Ideally the classroom should be provided with a central exhibition bench for use by the Instructor when using live exhibits.

Arrangement of curriculum

6 Classroom work should be arranged where possible between periods of active practical training.

Chapter 16

HEALTH OF DOGS

Introduction

1   The dog, being unable to speak, cannot explain to his handler or kennelman either that he is feeling ill or his symptoms. It is very important, therefore, that those having charge of dogs should be able to recognise the early warning signs of ill-health and also to describe the symptoms exhibited by the dog in order to assist the veterinary surgeon to make an accurate diagnosis. Early recognition and consequently early treatment of disease may well save a dog's life or stave off a serious epidemic. Each dog is an individual; what constitutes normal behaviour for one may be quite abnormal for another, so that the kennelman must know and understand each of the dogs in his care. It is important to remember that when a dog is ill or in pain, his training may be submerged by his wilder instincts and he may behave completely out of character. Consequently a good kennelman should be patient and tolerant, as well as observant. The frequency, colour and consistency of the bowel motions and the urine passed by each dog should be regularly checked as deviations from normal may indicate the onset of disease.

Calling in the veterinary surgeon

2   A handler or kennelman must never assume the duties of a veterinary surgeon as lay diagnosis and treatment are highly dangerous. In any case where the symptoms appear to denote a serious illness, or a condition where the use of drugs is obviously necessary, or where an apparently simple condition has failed to respond to simple remedies, then professional advice must be obtained without delay.

Nursing

3   Whilst the veterinary surgeon can do a great deal with the aid of modern drugs and surgical techniques to assist the dog's natural body defences to overcome the disease processes, rest and careful nursing are equally important to a successful outcome of an illness. The veterinary surgeon's instructions must be carefully followed, but the sick dog must be allowed as much rest as possible in quiet, warm and well-ventilated quarters secluded from his kennelmates. Where there is loss of appetite the dog should be tempted with his favourite titbits or careful handfeeding may be employed at the discretion of the veterinary surgeon. At all times the sick dog must be kept as clean as possible consistent with maximum rest. Any discharges must be carefully sponged away with warm water and a

little vaseline gently rubbed into the surrounding skin to avoid chapping or cracking.

Isolation

4 An isolation kennel should always be available so that in the event of a contagious or infectious disease being diagnosed, the affected animal may be quickly removed from contact with his fellows. Such a kennel should be able to withstand scrubbing of the floor and equipment with disinfectant solutions. A footbath of disinfectant should be kept at the entrance and, if possible, one attendant should confine himself to the care of the sick dog. If this is impossible the sick dog should be attended to last and the attendant should wear a plastice mac and rubber boots which can be washed down with disinfectant after leaving the isolation kennel.

Symptoms of illness

5 The following are symptoms of illness:-
   i)   Appetite (loss of): commonly indicates a stress factor, such as a chill or fever, over-work or training, stomach upset, etc. but may be the early signs of more serious disease.
   ii) Appetite (voracious): may indicate the presence of worms, or more serious conditions such as diabetes or pancreatic disease. It must be remembered that growing pups, bitches in whelp, or suckling pups normally show an increased appetite.
   iii) Breath (foetid): may be associated with stomach or bowel upsets, but is more commonly due to tartar on the teeth and inflammation of the gums. It may also be due to the presence of a decomposing piece of bone stuck between the teeth, but this is usually accompanied by obvious signs of mouth irritation. Tonsilitis, with accompanying painful swallowing, could be a cause and this may be an early sign of serious infectious disease, e.g. hardpad, distemper, etc. A urine-like odour of the breath denotes kidney disease and the smell of peardrops indicates diabetes.
   iv) Breathing (rapid): chill, fever, congestion of the lungs, bronchitis, pneumonia. May also indicate injury or shock or anaemia. In older dogs it is usually associated with heart disease.
   v)   Breathing (shallow): seen in shock, coma, and sometimes in painful conditions of the abdomen or chest. A gasping type of breathing is seen in cases of severe internal haemorrhage.
   vi) Constipation: this is usually due to lack of exercise or improper diet. Where the diet contains a high proportion of biscuits or where bones are fed, constipation frequently results. When the cessation of bowel function is accompanied by vomiting, veterinary advice should be obtained immediately.
   vii) Cough: inflammation of the throat or respiratory system generally, and is almost invariably present in hardpad and distemper. In the older dog it is a common sign of heart disease. In the puppy coughing may be due to worm infestation.
   viii) Diarrhoea: often due to stress, such as new environment, over-training, change of diet, etc. Unsuitable diet may also be a cause or worms or other internal parasites. Diarrhoea can be an early sign of infectious disease, or may indicate liver or pancreatic disease.

ix) Eyes: a watery discharge in both eyes turning to mucus and matter is present in distemper and to a lesser degree in hardpad. A similar condition may be seen in dogs which have been exposed to draughts, e.g. having their heads out of car windows. Inflammation in one eye may be due to injury or a foreign-body such as a grass seed. Occasionally one sees a grey opaque condition of the transparent part of the eye, with no accompanying discharge, and this may be due to viral hepatitis.

x) Nose: a dog's nose is normally cool and moist due to the evaporation of fluid produced by special glands in the skin of the area. In some diseases, particularly where there is a high temperature, the nose feels hot and dry, but this is by no means constant and it should only be regarded as a possible pointer to ill-health. In distemper and hardpad, the nose becomes caked with discharge and cracked, and in the latter disease one may see hardening and thickening of the skin of the nose.

xi) Temperature: the normal rectal temperature of the dog is 100–101°F in large dogs and 101–102 °F in the smaller breeds. The temperature is raised in infectious diseases, in painful conditions, or even when the dog is excited or nervous. The rectal temperature is a very important guide to a dog's condition and should be one of the first points to be checked when illness is suspected. If the dog is excited or nervous at the time of examination, re-check the temperature after a period of rest in a quiet kennel. The temperature may also fall below normal in some hormone deficiencies such as a sluggish thyroid gland, in circulatory collapse, e.g. shock, and when the dog is moribund (dying).

xii) Thirst: thirst is increased in various conditions. A high salt content of the diet, hot weather, vomiting and diarrhoea can all lead to an excessive water intake. Chronic kidney disease, heart disease and diabetes are serious diseases which are signalled by increased thirst.

xiii) Urine: variation in the frequency of urination, the amount and character of the urine passed are all important pointers to disease. Increased frequency, small quantities = cystitis (bladder inflammation). Increased frequency, large quantities = chronic kidney disease, diabetes. Decreased frequency = acute kidney disease, dehydration. Difficult or painful urination = bladder or urethral stones. Blood-stained urine, ammoniacal smell = cystitis or bladder stones. Deep yellow or orange-coloured urine = jaundice.

xiv) Vomiting: the dog is a vomiting creature and any condition which irritates the stomach may cause vomiting. For this reason, the occasional vomiting attack should not be regarded too seriously, but if vomiting persists or is frequent then veterinary advice should be obtained as soon as possible. Vomiting may be seen in infectious diseases such as distemper, jaundice, etc., in kidney disease, bowel obstruction, inflammation of stomach and bowels, and liver disease.

xv) Worms: generally speaking, round or threadworm infestation is seen in puppies, whereas the tapeworm is more commonly found in the adult dog. Puppies are often born with roundworms, being infected by their mother whilst still within the womb. The worms may not be seen but may pass out with the motion or be vomited up. A heavy worm burden may cause loss of condition, poor growth rate, diarrhoea, staring coat and potbelly, and occasionally fits. For complete eradication of the infestation, pups should be wormed at 14, 21 and 28 days after birth and again when 2 months old. Thereafter an annual dose should control the worms. It is important to prevent re-infection, so all faeces passed should be gathered up and burned as often as possible. Tapeworms have usually reached a state of balance with their host dog and neither party does the other very much harm. Tapeworms can be recognised by the appearance of small, yellowish-white segments, about the size of a cucumber seed, in the faeces or stuck to the hair around the anal region. The worms are very difficult to eradicate and treatment should only be carried out under the direction of the veterinary surgeon. A part of the life-cycle of the worm is spent in the flea and it is important to keep the dog free from these parasites.

General care

6 *Coat:* The dog should be groomed regularly to keep his coat in good condition. Grooming should be adequate without being excessive so as to preserve the dog's natural coat and watch should be kept for parasites, scratches or wounds which might need attention, as well as irritant substances which might cause skin trouble.

7 *Ears:* Ears should be examined from time to time for signs of inflammation, excessive wax production or discharges. *Probing of the ears must never be carried out except by the veterinary surgeon.* If cleaning is necessary the ears may be gently washed out with a warm soapy solution. Where the dog scratches his ear, shakes his head frequently, carries the ear down, or where there is a discharge, obtain veterinary attention as soon as possible.

8 *Feet:* A dog receiving regular exercise will generally keep his feet in good order without special attention from the handler, such as nail cutting, but a check should be kept on the length of the dewclaws as these do not wear down with contact with the ground. The feet should be inspected regularly for the presence of cysts between the toes and also for foreign bodies, such as grass seeds. Tar often collects on the hair between the pads and can cause eczema of the sensitive skin there if not removed. Sometimes mud gets caked on this hair to form hard balls which can cause lameness.

9 *Anus:* The dog has two anal glands, one at each side of the anus, approximately at the 4 and 8 o'clock positions. These are modified skin glands which produce a secretion. The glands are rather liable to become blocked, particularly in Alsatians, probably because of the down-pressed tail carriage. When this occurs there is quite a lot of irritation produced and the dog will rub its bottom on the ground, suddenly sit down and start up again quickly, look round at its tail end, or lick and bite at the tail root. If the condition is not relieved abscess formation may occur. The handler may be able to rectify the trouble by applying digital pressure on each side of the anal orifice at the positions mentioned above.

10 *Inoculations:* Vaccines are now available which will protect against all the common infections of the dog, viz, distemper, hardpad, virus hepatitis, lepto-spiral jaundice, parvo virus and leptospiral nephritis. The vaccine is given in two doses at a fortnightly interval, preferably when the puppy is 10-12 weeks old. The leptospiral fraction of the vaccine must be repeated annually and it is recommended that the virus vaccine should be boosted by a further dose at 2 years of age. The parvo virus vaccine should be repeated annually.

LARGE-SCALE ORGANISED SEARCHES

1 The following guiding principles for the use of police dogs in large-scale searches have been evolved by experience and are reproduced for the general information of supervising officers.

   i)   Irrespective of the total number of dogs and handlers which may be available for use, a team of 12 dogs is normally the maximum which can be properly co-ordinated at any one time.

   ii)   In normal conditions, a team of dogs and handlers should be capable of 4 consecutive hours' work. In extreme weather or over difficult terrain this capability will be reduced.

   iii)   A team relieved after one spell of searching is considered capable of re-employment after an interval of 4 hours provided in the interim they have been removed from the scene and given adequate rest and refreshment.

   iv)   The distance between the dogs will depend on the nature of the search – whether for a person or some item of property – as well as on the nature of the ground.

   v)   In searching for an escaped criminal, it is important that a straight line should be maintained. The distance between the dogs should not exceed 100 yards.

   vi)   When searching for property, the method of squaring the ground or box system should be adopted. The size of the 'box' will depend on the nature of the ground but should not exceed 100 yards frontage. Each dog should be required to work a 'box' in his own time in corridors which may be as narrow as 10 yards.

   vii)   Large-scale searches in built-up areas should follow the above principles but it may well be necessary to divide the area into pockets. The presence of officers intimately conversant with the locality is considered essential.

Communications

2 The maintenance of adequate communications with the searchers is essential. Ideally, for this purpose, every handler in the line of search over open country should be equipped with personal radio. The officer in charge of the dog team equipped with base station control should operate in a central position behind the search team. All should be under the radio control of the officer in charge of the operation at the Control van, outside the area to be searched. The latter should be in communication with Headquarters by radio or telephone.

3 In darkness or foggy weather, a small wrist compass should be carried by all personnel.

Briefing and operational procedure

4 Large-scale maps up to a scale of 25 inches to the mile are invaluable at the Control van. Each RT equipped searcher and all other RT personnel should be given an individual call-sign. Their relative positions should be shown on a master control plan and on plans held by the officer in charge of the dog team.

5 Preliminary briefing should include as much known information relative to the operation as is possible; subsequent briefing of developments and/or further instructions should be given by means of the RT equipment.

6 Searchers should be briefed to report by means of RT any find (property or bodies) and any other information likely to assist in the operation. Handlers should be instructed to remain at the scene of any find and to await the arrival of one of the link RT operators or other personnel detailed to attend. Articles of property should be clearly marked with detail of the place found and the spot marked with a small identifying stake. Such property should be taken to the Control van.

SCHEDULE OF TESTS AND NOTES FOR THE GUIDANCE OF JUDGES & COMPETITORS

The Tests will be divided into two parts as follows:

Part I   General Obedience and Criminal Work.
Part II   Nosework – Tracking and Searching.

Handlers who have been selected to officiate as judges at Regional or National Police Dog Trials, who are engaged fully with instructional duties, will not be eligible to compete.

All dogs taking part will be operational police dogs and will have qualified by having obtained the best marks in their respective District Trials and the dog obtaining the highest marks in the National Trials will be awarded the title "National Police Dog Champion".

In the event of a tie for placings, the position will be decided on the competitor obtaining the highest mark for the 'Hard Surface Track'. If there is a tie after this, the mark for the 'Two Hour Track' will be added.

In addition, certificates will be issued and graded at Regional Police Dog Trials as follows:

80% and over   Excellent
75–80%   Very Good
70–75%   Good
65–70%   Pass

Thus, in order to qualify for a certificate at Regional Trials, competitors must obtain at least 65% in Parts I and II. The grading of the certificates will be on the aggregate marks of all tests.

At National Police Dog Trials the first three competitors will be awarded appropriate certificates.

All other competitors will receive commemorative certificates.

The following schedule of tests and notes are for the guidance of Judges and competitors.

Part I   General obedience

For this exercise both Judges and competitors will wear uniform.

Test 1

(a) Heel free (Exercise)
The test will be carried out at a slow or normal walking pace, or at the double, as the Judge directs. The 'right', 'left', and 'about' turns are to be demonstrated at the command of the Judge. At each halt the dog will

Marks

25

remain in the 'stand' position at the command of the handler. Lateral deviations, running ahead, remaining behind, or sniffing, and repeated commands, will be penalised.

Notes for guidance. The dog will be required to walk readily and cheerfully at the left side of the handler with its right shoulder close to his left knee.

Slow, fast, and medium paces with 'right', 'left', and 'about' turns will be incorporated in the exercise.

The *'heel'* command will only be given when moving off from a stationary position.

Any method of influencing the dog to remain in the 'heel' position will be penalised.

Distractions will be included in the performance of this exercise.

(b) Send away, Re-Direction, and Distant Control (Exercise)
The dog will be required, upon command from the handler, to go to a specified point indicated by the Judge. This distance will not be less than 40 yards. Upon direction from the Judge, the dog will be sent to another specified point, being a distance of not less than 30 yards. This will be followed by the recall, during which the handler will be required to stop his dog in the 'stand' position. Distance control, the 'stand', 'sit' and 'down', will be carried out in any order as directed by the Judge. The recall will

50

then be completed, and followed by the finish to the 'heel' position.

Notes for Guidance. Where conditions allow, each dog should be sent to a different point. Maximum marks are to be allotted as follows:

Send away	15
Re-direction	15
Recall and distant control	15
Completion of exercise	5

(c) Retrieve (Exercise)
The dog will retrieve any article (excluding those made of glass or with a sharp edge) which, in the opinion of the Judge, it is likely to encounter when operational. The dog must not move forward to 'retrieve' or 'deliver to hand on return' until commanded to do so by the handler on direction

40

from the Judge.

Notes for guidance. The handler should take up a position with his dog leash free at the 'heel sit' and throw the article a distance not less than 15 yards. On direction from the Judge, the handler should send his dog to retrieve. The dog is required to go readily to the article, take it up at once without dropping it or mouthing it, and return quickly by the shortest route to the handler, taking up the 'sit' position in front of him. On further direction from the Judge, the handler should take hold of the article, giving the dog a command of *'leave'*. The dog is required to release the article immediately. The exercise is completed with the finish to the 'heel sit' position. The handler must not move his position during the whole exercise and extra commands will be penalised.

Articles should be practical and capable of being retrieved. **Marks**
Mouthing or dropping the article will be severely penalised.

(d) Agility
i   Obstacle Jump – three feet (Exercise)
The dog should be sent forward to clear the obstacle upon the command of
the handler, without touching it with its feet or hindquarters, and upon
further command, remain standing. The handler will be directed to rejoin
the dog, walk forward a few paces with the dog at 'heel' and thus complete
the exercise. The dog will be allowed one attempt only.   5

Notes for guidance. The handler should take up a position, at his own
discretion, in front of the jump with the dog 'heel free'. Upon command
the dog will be sent forward to clear the obstacle, without touching it with
its feet or hindquarters. Brushing with the tail will not be penalised. As
soon as the dog lands on the far side, it will be required to remain in the
'stand' position on command from the handler. On direction from the
Judge, the handler should rejoin the dog, walk forward a few paces with
the dog at 'heel', thus completing the exercise.

ii   Scramble board – six feet (Exercise)
Upon command from the handler, the dog will be sent forward to scramble
the obstacle, and on further command will remain stationary, in any
position, at the other side. At the direction of the Judge, the dog will be
recalled over the obstacle to rejoin its handler. The normal 'sit' in front of
the handler and the finish to 'heel' will be included in this exercise. The dog
will be allowed one attempt in either direction only.   30

Notes for guidance. The handler should take up a position, at his own
discretion, in front of the obstacle with the dog 'heel free', but having
taken up this position he must remain stationary until the exercise is
completed.
   Maximum marks will be awarded for each completed part of the test as
follows:
   Send over scramble board   10
   The stay   5
   Recall and completion of test   15

iii   Long Jump – nine feet (Exercise)
The dog will be required by the handler to clear the obstacle without
touching it with its feet or hindquarters and, upon further command,
remain at the 'stand'. The handler, upon direction from the Judge, will
then rejoin his dog and walk forward a few paces with the dog at 'heel'.
The exercise is then completed.   10

Notes for guidance. Consideration should be given to the placing of this
obstacle and to the use of suitable equipment.
   The handler will be allowed to take up any position he chooses, provided
it is not beyond the first unit of the jump, having first placed his dog in a
favourable position. Brushing the jump with the tail will not be penalised
and the dog will be allowed one attempt only.

Marks *(e) 'Speak' on command (Exercise)*

The handler will command or signal his dog to bark, under the direction of the Judge, and it should do so quite firmly. The dog should immediately respond to command or signal from the handler, and failure to do so, or **10** any undue assistance will be penalised.

This exercise is completed when the Judge is satisfied that the dog can 'speak', and cease to 'speak', on command.

(f) 'Down' handler out of sight (Exercise)

The dog will be required to remain in the 'down' position for the full period of 10 minutes, with the handler out of sight. The judge may cause the temperament of the dog to be tested by sending persons to walk round it, **20** or causing diversionary noises to be made.

Notes for guidance. The dog will be required to remain in the 'down' position for the full period with the handler out of sight and should not move until the Judge declares the exercise complete. All movements by the dog, other than easing into a more comfortable position, will be penalised, having regard to the stage in the exercise at which the infringement happened, or the circumstances of any infringement that may have occurred.

When leaving the dog only one command or signal will be allowed. If a dog moves more than 6 feet from the 'line' no marks will be awarded irrespective of the length of time it has remained in the original position, unless the movement be due to interference from another dog.

The Judge can remove a dog, the conduct of which, in his opinion, is likely to interfere with others engaged in the exercise.

(g) Test of steadiness to gun (Exercise)

The dog will walk heel free and two shots will be fired at a distance of **10** approximately 10 yards.

Notes for guidance. Although the dog is expected to take some interest when the shots are fired, it should remain steady, but undue apprehension or viciousness, or any leaving of the handler, will be penalised. Wherever possible the calibre of the gun should not be less than .32.

Total marks for Obedience   **200**

Part I Criminal work

For this exercise both judges and competitors will wear uniform.

Test 2

(a) Conduct of dog in crowds (Exercise)

This test will include general patrol amongst crowds, and the ability of the handler to deal with any specific incident that might occur during the patrol.

The dog will be required to remain under strict control, acting only on **60** specific commands from the handler.

Notes for guidance. This exercise is designed as the heading suggests, to test the conduct of the dog in varying crowd conditions.

At the direction of the Judge, the handler should patrol, with the dog at 'heel on leash', amongst an orderly crowd.

This will be followed by the handler and dog being required to arrest one or two disorderly persons within that crowd.

The temperament of the dog and the demeanour of the handler will be judged throughout the test.

Maximum marks will be allotted as follows:

Conduct of handler and dog in orderly crowd	10
Conduct of handler and dog whilst effecting arrest	25
Temperament of dog and demeanour of handler	25

(b) Chase and attack (Exercise)

The 'criminal' will run away, and on the direction of the Judge, the handler will order his dog to chase and attack. The attack will be done in a clean and determined manner, but without any undue excitement, viciousness, or apprehension. The dog must satisfy the Judge that he is capable of preventing the escape of a determined 'criminal'. If the 'criminal' escapes, no marks will be awarded.

After the attack, the search and escort of the 'prisoner' will be carried out.

100

Notes for guidance. The handler should take up a position with the dog leash free at 'heel'. The 'criminal', carrying some object or acting suspiciously, and at a distance of not less than 50 yards, when challenged by the handler will commence to run away. After a brief interval, during which the dog will be required to remain calm at the handler's side, the handler, upon direction of the Judge, will send the dog in pursuit. The dog is required to chase the 'criminal' at a brisk speed and stop him, by seizing an arm in a firm, clean and determined manner.

The 'criminal' should just sufficiently struggle to indicate to the Judge whether or not the dog is able to retain a firm hold. At the direction of the Judge, the handler will follow behind the dog and when approximately 10 yards away from the 'criminal', call it off. The dog is required to release immediately, either when the 'criminal' submits or upon a single command from the handler. The handler should then search the 'criminal' who should be positioned between himself and the dog at all times. After the search, the handler should escort the 'criminal' for a distance of not less than 50 yards in the direction of the Judge, with the dog in close proximity to the 'criminal'.

Failure to hold, viciousness, lack of control, or extra commands throughout the exercise, will be penalised. During the escort, the dog should be alert, and show that he has the 'criminal' under strict surveillance.

Maximum marks will be allotted as follows:

Chase and attack	65
Overall control	20
Search and escort	15

It is emphasised that whilst sufficient protection should be afforded the 'criminal', outer clothing worn on the arms should be loose enough for the dog to grip the clothing.

81

It is essential that the 'criminal' should be instructed to react in a similar manner, to ensure that all dogs are tested identically.

Marks

(c) Chase and stand-off (Exercise)
The dog will be required to chase, on command, a running person. This person will leave his place of concealment and commence to run away, thus arousing the handler's suspicions. The handler will, on the direction of the Judge, order his dog to chase. The running man, as the dog approaches, will stop and face the dog, whereupon the dog will circle and bark, and give clear indication that he is preventing the man's escape, until the arrival of the handler. Under no circumstances will the suspect attempt to escape once he is standing still. All undue excitement, viciousness, apprehension, or biting will be penalised. All additional commands will be penalised.

80

Notes for guidance. The handler should take up a position with the dog leash free at 'heel'. The suspect, acting suspiciously and at a distance of not less than 50 yards, when challenged by the handler will commence to run away. The dog will be required to remain calm at the handler's side until directions are received from the Judge to send the dog in pursuit. The dog will be required to chase after the suspect at a brisk speed. The command given to the dog must be exactly the same as the one for the 'chase and attack' exercise. When the dog is about 20 yards away, the suspect will stop, turn about, and face the dog. The dog must not bite but will keep the suspect under strict surveillance until the arrival of the handler.

It will give tongue spontaneously and consistently and, at the same time, circle the suspect in a firm and determined manner. On direction from the Judge the handler will take up a position approximately 10 yards from the suspect. He will then call the dog out by giving one command and place it in a strategic position. The handler will then approach the suspect, interrogate him, and upon being satisfied, release him as an inncoent person. Whilst the suspect walks away, the handler should call the dog to heel and walk in a different direction.

No stick or other means of provocation are to be used by the suspect, and biting, or lack of control, will be penalised. After the release of the dog, any additional command will be penalised by the deduction of 15 marks.

Maximum marks to be allotted are as follows:

Chase and stand off and surveillance	45
Overall control	15
Circle and bark	20

(d) Test of courage

i Stick (Exercise)
The dog will be required to engage a 'criminal' armed with a stick which is used to deter the attack. The dog will make a spontaneous and determined attack and any encouragement by the handler will be penalised.

30

Notes for guidance. The dog will 'hold' the 'criminal' in a determined manner, without endangering itself, until the 'criminal' has been disarmed by the handler. When the 'criminal' has been disarmed, with one

command the handler will cause his dog to leave and will place it in a **Marks**
strategic position. The dog will be required to engage the 'criminal' without
the assistance of its handler, until the Judge is satisfied that its courage has
been fully tested. Failure to make a determined attack, lack of courage,
becoming endangered, or extra commands will be penalised. Particular
attention should be paid to the selection of suitable sticks in this exercise,
(bamboo canes are recommended), and in any case they should not exceed
4 feet in length and $\frac{1}{2}$ inch diameter.

Maximum marks to be allotted are as follows:

Courage of the dog 20
Control of dog and action of handler 10

The dog will be required to resolutely attack a 'criminal' armed with a
gun, regardless of gunfire and without undue viciousness or apprehension. **30**

Notes for guidance. The dog will make a spontaneous and determined
attack, and any encouragement by the handler will be penalised. The dog
will 'hold' the 'criminal' in a determined manner until he has been
disarmed by the handler. When the 'criminal' has been disarmed, with one
command the handler will cause his dog to be placed in a strategic position.
Failure to make a determined attack, lack of courage, or extra commands
will be penalised. Wherever possible, the calibre of the weapon should not
be less than .32.

Maximum marks to be allotted are as follows:

Courage of the dog 20
Control of dog and action of handler 10

NB In Part I, Test 2(b), (c) and (d), and in Part II, Test 2(c), the
suspect/criminal will not wear any visible means of protection.

Total marks for Criminal Work **300**

During the period of the Trials all competitors and their dogs are barred
from all Part I test areas, and the use of the equipment, except whilst they
are actually being tested.

However, there will be no objection to them being spectators. Judges of
Part I Exercises will pay particular attention to the demeanor and
policemanship of the handler.

Part II Nosework: tracking and searching

Test 1

(a) Track (Exercise)
Leash track, about half-a-mile long and approximately 2 hours old, to be
laid by an experienced person, other than the handler. Four track layer's
articles will be dropped on the track. The conclusion of the track will be
indicated by an inconspicuous marker, approximately 20 yards after the
last article. No marks will be awarded for the additional article. Running
when working the track will be penalised. The area from which the track
starts will be clearly marked. The handler will inform the Judge prior to the

Marks
140 commencement of the track the method in which the dog will indicate each article.

Notes for guidance. All tracks, as far as possible, should be laid under similar conditions, although a variety of terrain may be introduced. They will be planned in advance, and it is essential that experienced men be employed as track layers.

Careful consideration should be given to the selection of articles, so that they are in keeping with the type of ground over which the dog is expected to work. The articles must have been in the personal possession of the track layer for at least half an hour, but not kept in any type of container.

The track will start from a square clearly marked with 4 pegs each 20 yards apart. The tracks should be laid in a normal walking pattern and 'scuffing' will not be permitted. The articles to be found will be placed inconspicuously in the same sequence on each track. They will neither be deliberately concealed nor positioned near a bend or turn.

The dog may be praised and encouraged as often as desired, but any other influence is forbidden.

Upon finding the article, the dog must give a positive indication and remain stationary until the article has been recovered by the handler. The handler will indicate the finding of the article by raising his arm to the Judge, who will acknowledge the signal. No recast by the Judge is allowed. However, should the handler recast the dog at his own discretion, he will be allowed to continue. Should the dog lose the track and appear likely to foul another track, or the allotted time expires, the handler and dog will be called off. If, in the opinion of the Judge, the dog is lost beyond recovery of the track, he is entitled to conclude the test. When the dog reaches the final marker the test is completed and no recasting will be allowed.

Maximum marks to be allotted are as follows:

Method of working and handling the dog   20
Working the track   80

Each article carries 10 marks for correct indication and recovery by the dog. Should the article be otherwise recovered, 5 marks will be awarded. A maximum of 20 minutes will be allowed for this exercise.

(b) Hard surface track (Exercise)
The track will be laid on hard surface. The track will be approximately half an hour old, and not more than half a mile long. One track layer's article will be dropped on the track.

Running when working the track will be penalised. The handler will inform the Judge prior to the commencement of the track the method in which the dog will indicate each article.

140

Notes for Guidance. All tracks, as far as possible, should be laid under similar conditions, although a variety of terrain may be introduced into each track.

The track should be laid in a normal walking pattern and 'scuffing' is not permitted. Tracks will be planned in advance, and it is essential that experienced men be employed as track layers. Careful consideration should be given to the selection of the article, so that it is in keeping with

the type of ground over which the dog is expected to work. The article **Marks**
must have been in the personal possession of the track layer for at least half
an hour, but not kept in any type of container.

The article to be found will be placed inconspicuously at the end of the
track.

Running when working the track will be penalised. The dog may be
praised and encouraged as often as desired, but any other influence is
forbidden.

Upon finding the article, the dog must give a positive indication and
remain stationary until the article has been recovered by the handler. The
handler will indicate the finding of the article by raising his arm to the
Judge, who will acknowledge the signal. No recast by the Judge is allowed.
However, should the handler recast the dog at his own discretion, he will
be allowed to continue.

Should the dog lose the track and appear likely to foul another track, or
the time allotted expires, the handler and the dog will be called off. If, in
the opinion of the Judge, the dog is lost beyond recovery of the track, he is
entitled to conclude the test. When the dog reaches the final marker the
test is complete.

Time to be allowed for this exercise is 20 minutes.

Maximum marks to be allotted as follows:
    Method of working and handling dog   20
    Working the track   100

The article carries 20 marks for correct indication and recovery by the
dog. Should the article be otherwise recovered, 10 marks only will be
awarded.

Competitors should at no time be on the tracking grounds until they are
required to compete.

(c) Police work (Separate Exercise)   **80**
Notes for guidance. The test (c) will be judged on the ability of the handler
to work at an incident requiring police investigation, and should be staged
in a practical manner and not merely as a classroom incident.

He will be judged on his interrogation of possible witnesses, his
demeanour, his powers of observation and actions he will take preparatory
to putting his dog to work.

Time allowed for this exercise will be 15 minutes.

Total marks for Tracking   360

Part 2 Searching

Test 2

(a) Searching for property (Exercise)
The dog will be required to search and find, in a defined area, 3 specific
articles bearing scent. The 3 articles are to be retrieved.

Careful consideration should be given to the selection of articles, so that
they are in keeping with the type of ground over which the dog is expected
to work.

85

The search area will not exceed 25 yards square and the handler, whilst free to exercise discretion as to his own positioning, must not actually enter the area.

50   Seven minutes will be allowed for this test.

Notes for guidance. The above articles will bear a stranger's scent and will be placed in the area approximately half an hour prior to the commencement of the search.

The articles will be of the same type and size, but different articles will be used for each competitor.

They must have been in the personal possession of the Steward for at least half an hour, but not kept in any type of container.

The area used should be walked over prior to the article being placed, and similarity in this respect should be maintained.

Whenever possible separate areas should be provided for each dog.

The time allowed for this test is 7 minutes which will commence from the conclusion of the briefing. The dog should work the whole area in a methodical manner and always under control.

The handler is not allowed to enter the area.

     Articles (12 for each)   36
     Method of working dog   14

(b) Indication of an irretrievable article (Exercise)

The dog is required to search for and find an irretrievable article and

20   indicate its presence by barking.

Notes for guidance. This exercise is designed to test the ability of the dog to locate and indicate an irretrievable article. The article will be placed out of sight of the dog and handler and, where possible, it will be placed in a different area for each dog.

The dog will be required to search for the article and indicate its presence by barking. The handler, after the initial command and release of the dog, will be allowed to encourage it until such time as it becomes obvious that the dog has located the article.

However, he will not use words of encouragement which include the command *'speak'*.

The dog will remain with the article until the Judge is satisfied that it has completed the exercise to his satisfaction. Upon direction from the Judge the handler will rejoin his dog and recover the article.

Maximum time allowed is 5 minutes.

Maximum marks to be allotted are as follows:

     Indication   15
     Method of working dog   5

(c) Quarter and search for hidden person (Exercise).

This test may be carried out in a building, yard or open space. The dog must methodically quarter and search the area or building thoroughly and bark on finding the hidden person.

70   Leaving or attacking the hidden person will be penalised.

Notes for guidance. OPEN YARD OR OPEN SPACE. The dog is required to
quarter and search the area in a methodical manner and always under
control.

Special attention will be paid to the handler's ability to direct his dog
from one place to another, until it is obvious that the dog has located the
scent of the hidden person.

On finding, a clear indication should be given by barking. Biting will be
heavily penalised and the dog should remain with the hidden person until
the arrival of the handler.

SEARCH OF A BUILDING OR CONGESTED PLANTATIONS. The dog will be
required to quarter and search the area in a methodical manner. The
handler, after the initial command and release of the dog, will be allowed
to encourage his dog until such time as it has given a clear indication that it
has located the scent of the hidden person by barking. However, he will
not use words of encouragement which include the command *'speak'*.
When the dog has indicated the hidden person by barking, further
commands and encouragement will be penalised. Biting will be penalised
and the dog should remain with the hidden person until the arrival of the
handler.

When the test is carried out in an area or building in which it is
impossible for Judges to keep the dog in full view at all times, one of the
Judges will act as the hidden person so that the dog's reactions and work
can be fully assessed.

On these occasions the aggregate marks for the test will be awarded after
the Judges have compared notes. It is important that during this exercise
the minimum amount of protective clothing be used, and in any case must
not be visible to the dog.

Dependent upon the type of area or building which has to be worked,
reasonable time should be allowed by the Judge for this exercise.

The allotted time will not exceed 15 minutes.

Maximum marks to be allotted are as follows:

Method of searching   25
Finding hidden person   45

In this exercise the Judge will always take into consideration the method
and amount of searching done by the dog and will mark accordingly.

Total marks for Searching   140

Schedule of marks

Part 1   General obedience

Test 1

a	Heel, free	25
b	Send away, re-direction and distant control	50
c	Retrieve article	40
d	Agility: Obstacle	5
	Scale	30
	Long jump	10
e	'Speak' on command	10
f	'Down' handler out of sight	20
g	Steadiness to gun	10

Total 200

Total marks for Part 1: 500

Part 2   Tracking

Test 1

a	Track	140
b	Hard surface track	140
c	Police work	80

Total 360

Total Marks for Part II: 500

Part 1   Criminal work

Test 2

a	Conduct of dog in crowds	60
b	Chase and attack	100
c	Chase and stand-off	80
d	Test of courage: Stick	30
	Gun	30

Total 300

Part 2   Searching

Test 2

a	Searching for property	50
b	Indication of an irretrievable article	20
c	Quarter and search for hidden person	70

Total 140

SYLLABUS FOR PUPPY TRAINING

Syllabus of puppy allocation course, monthly visits to Dog Training Establishment and one week's training at the age of nine months.

Metropolitan Police
Puppy allocation course 3 days

	DAY ONE	TWO	THREE
8.30 am	Report to DTE ALLOCATE LOCKERS Introduce to puppies and puppy kennel area.	Clean kennels and area. Feed and exercise pups.	Clean kennels and area. Feed and exercise pups.
9.15 am	BREAK	BREAK	BREAK
9.30 am	CLASSROOM. Rules of DTE DOCUMENTATION OF HANDLERS.	LECTURE. Grooming, daily examination of puppy and hygiene.	LECTURE. Canine first aid. Veterinary procedure. Settling puppy into home environment with kennelling advice.
10.15 am	ALLOCATE PUPPIES	Visit local residential area with pups for short ride in vehicle and walk.	QUESTIONS
10.45 am	Complete documentation. Give handlers details of puppies' breeding and history.	Practical grooming and examination of pups.	Practical grooming and examination of pups.
11.40 am	Exercise and feed pups.	Feed	Feed
12 noon	BREAK	BREAK	BREAK
1.00 p.m.	LECTURE feeding of puppy	LECTURE. physical and mental development of pup.	Allocation of vitamins etc., to last puppy for 4 weeks. Cleaning and disinfecting of kennel.
2.30 pm	Exercise puppies. Clean kennels. Feed puppies.	As previous day.	Talk by Chief Superintendent.
3.30 pm	Dismiss	Dismiss	Dismiss to homes with puppies.

All puppies, whether bred at the Dog Training Establishment or acquired from outside, are treated in the same way regarding allocation, walking and pre-basic course training.

Puppies at the age of 12 weeks, or if when acquired over 12 weeks and under one year, are allocated to handlers. The allocation consists of a 3 day course, syllabus as follows. The puppies are then taken home by the handlers under the Puppy Walking Scheme to be developed and trained, where desirable, in preparation for the basic training course. It is intended that the man rearing the puppy will eventually attend the basic training course with that puppy and be its handler.

Schedule of puppy visits to D.T.E. one day each month

Age at Visit	
4 months	Weighing of puppy. Examination and assessment of development. Discussion with handlers regarding any problems. Advice on next month's requirements. Issue of monthly supply of vitamins as necessary.
5 months	As above. Instruction regarding development and encouragement of desirable attributes and discouragement of undesirable traits.
6 months	As above. Instruction regarding *gentle* obedience. Training with emphasis on pitfalls of over compulsion. Development rather than compulsion. 'Walk to heel', 'sit', leave in sit, play retrieve, play clothwork.
7 months	As above. All round progress noted. Recall introduced from 'Sit', 'Stand' and leave in stand.
8 months	As above. Continued development of gentle obedience. 'Heel', 'Sit', 'Stand', 'Retrieve', 'Recall', Play with cloth.
9 months	Five day course at D.T.E. See syllabus.
10 months	As at all visits, assess development and suitability of dog and handler. Practise all exercises taught and advise regarding development of exercises.
11 months	As for 10 months. Advise handler as to dates of Basic Course. With full co-operation of handler and correct development the puppy should, before attending Basic Course, 'walk to heel' on and off leash, recall to front and to 'heel'. Retrieve, be agile. Track about 20 minutes old at 200 yards. Bite fairly firmly on loose cloth on Instructor's arm. 'Speak' on Command and at suspicious persons when encouraged. 'Sit', 'Stand', 'Down', when told and remain in position.

Care must be taken throughout the walking period that over compulsion is not used and that the development is within the puppy's physical and mental capabilities. It is found necessary to adjust the Schedule for some individual puppies in order not to overtax them.

The period is designed as a preparation for the Basic Course and could never replace it.

Syllabus for five day's training of puppies at the age of nine months

TIME	MONDAY	TUESDAY	WEDNESDAY	THURSDAY	FRIDAY
8.30 am to 9.00 am	Allocate kennels. Assembly.	Exercise, groom dogs. Clean kennels.	Exercise, groom dogs. Clean kennels.	Exercise, groom dogs. Clean kennels.	Exercise, groom dogs. Clean kennels.
9.30 am to 12 noon	CLASSROOM Introduction to Course by Supt. RULES OF D.T.E. Question as to behaviour of dogs at home and under various circumstances.	CLASSROOM Basic principles of training.	COMMENCE ELEMENTARY TRACKING Demonstrate 'sit'. Practise all exercises taught.	Elementary tracking. Agility. Practise control.	Elementary tracking. Agility. Practise control. Introduce 'down'.
12 noon to 1.00 pm			LUNCH		
1.00 pm to 3.00 pm	Assessment of dog's physical and character development. Light training to note co-ordination between dog and handler.	Demonstrate: 'Heelwork'. 'Stand'. 'Retrieve'. Practise all above exercises.	Elementary biting cloth. 'Speak' at concealed person. Practise all control exercises so far taught.	Demonstrate property search. Biting cloth, speaking as required by individual.	CLASSROOM Discussion on Course. Explain development of all exercises taught. TALK BY CHIEF SUPERINTENDENT
3.00 pm	Feed dogs. Bed dogs down. Clean kennel surrounds.	Feed dogs. Bed dogs down. Clean kennel surrounds.	Feed dogs. Bed dogs down. Clean kennel surrounds.	Feed dogs. Bed dogs down. Clean kennel surrounds.	Feed dogs. Bed dogs down. Clean kennel surrounds.
5.00 pm			DISMISS		

Basic training schedule

It will be understood that where a dog has been developed under the Puppy Training Syllabus the 1st and 2nd weeks' training as shown hereunder will not normally apply.

Week 1

Exercise and gaining confidence of dogs. Elementary heel work and introducing the 'sit' and 'down'. The Instructor must be most insistent on correct leash work, pointing out the faults immediately. This is the basis on which all future control depends. Continually demonstrate the difference between the pull and jerk. The 'down' must be gentle for some weeks. Importance of praise emphasised.

Week 2

Heel work, 'sit', 'down', and introducing the 'leave'. (Plenty of individual work, rather than as a class.) Elementary controlled jumping. Elementary steps in the 'retrieve', the 'speak' and *holding the cloth'*. (It is important that dogs are not excited in these exercises. Keep dog as calm as possible.) Leash track introduced, laid by handler.

LECTURES

1 Equipment and care of same.
2 Care of dog. Examination and grooming.
3 Introduction to training and central principles involved.
4 Temperament and formation of dog.
5 Feeding and hygiene.

Week 3
Continued build up of above obedience exercises, but only in short periods.
Introducing leash tracks laid by Instructor with article at end. Then on to harness and leash.
Remember never rush the distance of these tracks. A gradual build up of time and distance is essential. Jumping and retrieving. Speaking at concealed person and the cloth.

LECTURES

6   The theories of scent.

7   Tracking.

Week 4
The first 4 weeks are devoted to the handler gradually gaining control over the dog in all exercises. This is to be done by affection and firmness, but never by brutality. The Instructor can be responsible for the success or failure of the dogs and handlers. He must exercise rigid discipline in demanding correct training and must always act as teacher in all track laying and man work exercises.

HEEL WORK	Dogs to walk correctly at heel in a quiet manner under all circumstances. (Do not have too many turns and vary the pace.) Dogs to be able to 'sit' and 'down' on leash.
LEAVE	This should be first done on leash then gradually leave. Only go to front and go to correct side. Never go in a circle behind the dog as it may pull him off the 'leave' position.
TRACKING	To successfully follow a fairly simple track and find articles.
SEEKING	To readily 'speak' at criminal. This exercise needs constant practise. Actual seeking is preferably done at this stage in a building.
RETRIEVE	This is a most important exercise and should be concentrated upon, but only for short periods.
CHASING	To grip and hold fast onto *trainer's* right arm. Once you have the dog doing this firmly, cease this exercise until the last 4 weeks.

LECTURE

8   Criminal work.

During the first 4 weeks it is essential that the handler is always in a position to immediately enforce all commands given to the dog. Therefore, the dog must be on the leash in the teaching of all the exercises during this period. Gunfire from a distance must be introduced in a careful manner.

Week 5

CONTROL	Further development of training previously given. Recall from the 'sit' position is introduced.
TRACKING	Gradual increase of age of tracks. Various surfaces.
SEEKING	Free seeks only in buildings. Concentrate on the 'speak'.
RETRIEVE	Different articles to be introduced. Remember searching for hidden articles. (Not too difficult.)
CHASING	Continued build up of weaker dogs. *Distant* gunfire. Controlled jumping over *gradually* increasing heights.

LECTURE

9   History of dog. Understanding between man and dog.

Week 6

CONTROL	The weak points of both handlers and dogs to be concentrated upon. Long jump introduced.

TRACKING	*Gradual* build up over all surfaces (soft) both in length and time.
SEEKING	In buildings free. Hidden persons for dog to 'speak' on scent. Plenty of practice in the 'speak'. Get them to bark for increasing lengths of time. Different 'criminals' may be used.

LECTURE

10   The correct use of dog in police work.

Week 7

CONTROL	Practice all exercises both as a class and individually.
RETRIEVE	Continue to build up.
TRACKING	A continued build up of length and time lags. Small objects to be found by scent and not sight.
SEEKING	Seeking free in woods to be introduced.
SCALE	Elementary scale jumping. Remember height and distance.

Week 8

CONTROL	Continued build up. 'Retrieve' with assorted articles. Jumping and scale. *Never too much of this exercise as it is a strain and very tiring.*
TRACKING	Introduction of good dogs to hard surfaces.
SEEKING	Development of seeking. Dog to remain for increasing periods with person hidden, and give tongue freely. Concentrate on this 'speak'.

Week 9

CONTROL	Concentrate in small doses on all exercises taught. Introduction drop on recall to all fast moving dogs.
TRACKING	Keep to all surfaces including road.
SEEKING	Continuance of 'seek' exercises. Practice of retrieve of all types of articles and a few minutes jumping each day. (Not for too long a period.)

LECTURES

11   Police order relating to dogs, railway memorandum and other dangers likely to be met operationally. Use of dogs in connection with rowdyism and crowds.
12   The importance of continuity training in the education of the dog.

Weeks 5, 6, 7, 8 and 9 are to be devoted to the furtherance of the handler's control over his dog in all circumstances. The recall is introduced in obedience from the 'sit' position, although of course this has already been done in the 'retrieve', 'seek' and 'chasing'.
Do not recall from the 'down' position at this stage. Leaving out of sight also comes at this phase. The dogs are taught to jump various natural obstacles. Not too much or too high.

TRACKING: This exercise should be steadily built up, both in length and time lag. The dogs should be taught to track at a steady speed and remain on a given scent. Remember elementary road tracking should be given, but only with a short time lag.

SEEKING: The dog should find and remain with the 'criminal' until arrival of handler. Any inclination to attack must be cured. All dogs should by now have been built up to tackle firmly on road and soft surfaces. Avoid boring dogs with too long lessons, especially in obedience, retrieve and jumping.

Week 10

CONTROL	Practise all exercises so far taught. Aim now for smartness and correct performance. Introduce the 'stay', (i.e. the 'stand at heel'). Introduce the advanced and sterner method of dropping the dog.

RETRIEVE	Soft, hard and metal objects. Searching for articles. Nose only.
AGILITY	Introduce the sending forward, 'over' and 'stay'.
TRACKING	Time lag and length continually increased. Majority of tracks on hard surfaces with cross tracks.
SEEKING	Continued build up with special attention to control. Factory yards and buildings.
CHASING	This exercise should be re-introduced. Control on the finish must be aimed at.

Week 11

CONTROL	All exercises practised in short lessons.
AGILITY	Gradually increasing heights but great care must be taken not to strain the dogs.
TRACKING	Road tracking with junctions.
SEEKING	Squaring and double seek.
CHASING	As previous week. Special attention to escorting prisoners. Chase to be done through crowds.
	TEST ONE TO BE COMPLETED THIS WEEK.

Week 12

CONTROL	Frequent exercises to be done in different surroundings.
AGILITY	Practise in short lessons.
RETRIEVE	Practise in short lessons.
TRACKING	Angled tracks of one hour time lag.
SEEKING	Concentration of correct seeking in all types of surroundings. Build up of all other exercises.
	TEST TWO TO BE COMPLETED THIS WEEK.

Weeks 13 and 14

Test three and final test to be given. These 2 weeks must be spent in overcoming any faults the dogs may have. Practical tests will be devised for various classes. By the end of the course, all the dogs, though young and immature, should have a *solid foundation* in the following exercises.

A LEASH WORK	Correct performance required.
B FREE HEEL	Correct performance required.
C OBEDIENCE	Correct performance required.
D TRACKING	A minimum time lag of one hour is required — 2 articles to be found.
E SEEKING	To square an area, find and give tongue at a wanted person.
F CHASING	To tackle right arm and *hold*. Absolute control required. Off leash.
G SEARCHING	To search an area and find property. Under control.
H JUMPING	To jump and scale such heights and obstacles as is consistent with age of the dog.
I RETRIEVE	To carry all types of articles.
NOTES	*Made at morning discussion.*
A RETRIEVE	*Must retrieve dumb-bell for 'GOOD'. In good performance.*
B	*Correct.* *'Sit' 2 minutes. 'Down' 10 minutes.* *'Stand'. 'Down' 'sit' recall.*
D E F	*Correct.*
G	*22 yards square, 3 articles, 5 minutes. Correct.*

94

Printed in the UK for HMSO
Dd 718715/C25/5/83/LoM